Praise for *Connect and Involve:*
How to Connect With Students and Involve Them in Learning

"This is a great read! I initially read *Connect and Involve* with the idea of taking copious notes regarding the manuscript before writing my commentary. However, I became so intrigued by the message and organization of the book that I forgot to take notes, and I read the manuscript a second time. Dr. Martin presents a valuable compendium of proven techniques, ideas, and resources with a commonsense approach to active student learning. Too often educators try to be 'all things to all students.' Dr. Martin reminds us to only do what we can control and to focus on what is important. I wholeheartedly believe that *Connect and Involve* is the quintessential primer for all educators, especially for veteran teachers who mentor new educators."

—**Dr. Janie Theobald**, retired elementary school principal and veteran elementary, middle, and high school teacher, including special education

"I am absolutely loving it! I love how Martin's book really homes in on key elements that all teachers should focus on. It is a great reminder to seasoned teachers and it is a fantastic guide to new teachers on motivating and involving students in their own education. I appreciate that there is the ability to choose a particular area to focus on and utilize that chapter to improve my students' environment and education, which is important for busy educators! An excellent resource for every classroom!"

—**Nicole Marshall**, fourth grade teacher with nineteen years' experience

"What a prize text! I found solutions to the problems plaguing our classrooms and data teams in Martin's procedures and strategies—simple ideas that implemented immediately will impact whole-class learning and address individual struggling students' needs. This is research and best practice translated into the 'boots on the ground' movement. I've already begun to use ideas from the text with my Building Leadership Team in building a quality MTSS, pulled out strategies and teaching procedures to help in drafting a 504 plan for a student with ADHD, worked in a student action team meeting to help build relationships through reframing teacher thinking, and worked on identifying and fulfilling student needs."

—**Suzann Copeland**, school examiner and veteran elementary school teacher

"*Connect and Involve* speaks to my heart as a teacher. I think it is the kind of book that will speak to the hearts of all educators. There is nothing trendy about the techniques—no fleeting terminology that is going to fall out of

favor before the book even has a chance to be read through cover to cover. By the same token, there is also not a single technique or idea that is unadventurous or overly conventional. Dr. Martin lands squarely on the gold standard by streamlining universal best practice. Whether you are a preservice teacher in training, a brand-new classroom teacher, or a seasoned educator, this book is full of effective strategies you can readily and simply implement in your practice. That, I think, is what all of us want as teachers . . . simple ideas and tools to help us do an even better job reaching and teaching our students."
—**Loddie Krepps**, twenty-seven-year veteran middle and high school English teacher, reading specialist, and special education teacher

"*Connect and Involve* is an accessible road map for teachers and others to implement highly engaging techniques into their professional practices. In this age of diminishing and even impoverished choices for students and those who work with them, the skills, strategies, and best practices throughout the book are truly welcomed. I highly recommend this book."
—**Dr. Sam Minner**, president of New Mexico Highlands University and former public school teacher

"An exceptional addition to the library of any educator who is truly dedicated to improving connections/relationships with students and thus improving not only their academic achievement but their lives and future opportunities. Martin synthesizes his more than forty years' experience as a psychologist and educator into one comprehensive and cohesive guide which provides timely, real-world actions and behaviors focused on improving relationships with students as a means to enhance their learning and academic achievement. The strategies and practices in this book align well the work of Chappuis, Marzano, Hattie, and others regarding what works in classrooms and solidifies the position that enhanced student learning and achievement hinges not only on good teaching practice but on positive, meaningful relationships with students."
—**James F. Judd**, director of the Northeast Missouri Regional Professional Development Center and former superintendent and public school teacher

"This outstanding handbook is intuitive for both beginning teachers and veterans of many years because it encourages these educators to make small, practical changes that yield big payoffs. The chapters are cohesive and connected but can also stand alone if an educator is looking for a particular strategy. Question-and-answer sections at the end of each chapter thoughtfully review the material while providing additional classroom applications. Dr. Martin's book draws heavily on his expertise and years of experience working with K–12 students and educators. *Connect and Involve* is sure to become one of an educator's most trusted resources."

—**Jeanne Harding**, veteran elementary and gifted education teacher, elementary principal, and current director of preservice education field experiences and interim dean at Truman State University

"*Connect and Involve* is content rich and loaded with practical information that a preservice teacher or a practicing teacher can find applicable. Robert Martin's enthusiasm for teaching and learning is clearly evident throughout the text—and he shares strategies that stand the test of time. The question-and-answer sections at the end of each chapter are very helpful. When reading, I found myself revisiting strategies that I had used previously but had not articulated well. Dr. Martin's ability to make the complexity of learning and teaching accessible to readers is extremely helpful. This is a text you will enjoy reading."

—**Wendy Miner**, department chair and professor of education at Truman State University and veteran teacher of almost all grade levels, including fourth grade, fifth-grade gifted program, and sixth-grade science

Connect and Involve

How to Connect with Students and Involve Them in Learning

Dr. Robert J. Martin

Foreword by Carleen Glasser,
President of William Glasser, Inc.

ROWMAN & LITTLEFIELD
Lanham • Boulder • New York • London

Published by Rowman & Littlefield
An imprint of The Rowman & Littlefield Publishing Group, Inc.
4501 Forbes Boulevard, Suite 200, Lanham, Maryland 20706
www.rowman.com

6 Tinworth Street, London SE11 5AL, United Kingdom

Copyright © 2020 by Robert J. Martin

All rights reserved. No part of this book may be reproduced in any form or by any electronic or mechanical means, including information storage and retrieval systems, without written permission from the publisher, except by a reviewer who may quote passages in a review.

British Library Cataloguing in Publication Information Available

Library of Congress Cataloging-in-Publication Data

Names: Martin, Robert J., 1944- author. | Glasser, Carleen, writer of foreword.
Title: Connect and involve : how to connect with students and involve them in learning / Robert J. Martin ; foreword by Carleen Glasser.
Description: Lanham : Rowman & Littlefield, [2020] | Includes bibliographical references and index.
Identifiers: LCCN 2020004565 (print) | LCCN 2020004566 (ebook) | ISBN 9781475857603 (cloth) | ISBN 9781475857610 (paperback) | ISBN 9781475857627 (epub)
Subjects: LCSH: Effective teaching. | Teacher effectiveness. | Teacher-student relationships. | Curriculum planning.
Classification: LCC LB1025.3 .M33718 2020 (print) | LCC LB1025.3 (ebook) | DDC 371.102—dc23
LC record available at https://lccn.loc.gov/2020004565
LC ebook record available at https://lccn.loc.gov/2020004566

To William Glasser, MD, who led by example,
showing that we learn to teach students
by working with them until we learn how

Contents

Foreword		xi
Preface		xii
Acknowledgments		xvii
1	Make Small Changes	1
2	Connect Through Getting to Know Students	11
3	Connect Through Helping Students Make Choices	25
4	Design Learning Starting From the Big Ideas and Key Skills	37
5	Design Lessons Starting From the Big Content Ideas and Key Skills	49
6	Use Scoring Guides to Increase Quality Work	57
7	Motivation Follows Action	67
8	Increase Learning by Teaching Procedures	79
9	Help Students Learn Through Practice and Revision	89
10	Use Teams to Increase Practice	101
11	Plan Projects That Use Teams	113
12	Use Conversation to Increase Learning and Build Community	125

13	Involve Students in Your Presentations	135
Afterword		147
References		149
Index		155
About the Author		161

Foreword

I am very impressed with this book. As soon as teachers begin to implement the groundbreaking ideas in this book, they could literally change the face of education today for the better. Dr. Robert Martin offers clear and easy-to-understand explanations, showing teachers how to connect with students by creating a needs-satisfying environment in the classroom. William Glasser, MD, proposed that all behavior is driven internally by five basic needs: survival, love and belonging, power, freedom, and fun. Dr. Martin gives teachers strategies and procedures in this book to reach every student by getting to know them, involving them in learning, and helping them increase their achievement.

Glasser recommends class meetings where students engage in conversations that increase learning and build community. Likewise, in *Connect and Involve*, readers also learn to plan projects that use teams and connect students through helping them make effective choices. Martin explains further using the reflective practitioner model of learning something new: First the students are given a task to do, then they observe what happens, then reflect on changes, and finally make new choices. This and many other useful ideas to make teaching a joy will keep the reader involved in learning new and unique approaches to effective teaching that can be used immediately in any classroom.

Carleen Glasser, President, William Glasser, Inc.
Senior Faculty, William Glasser Institute
Retired Elementary and High School Art Teacher
and Elementary and High School Counselor

Preface
Make a Small Change

When I was a senior in high school, one of my teachers, an experienced teacher in his sixties, was a bit of a mystery to me. The course involved a small group preparing translations of Latin classics and then working through them in class, each of us taking a turn. I asked how he could teach the same authors and texts year after year. His answer was simple: Every year, the students are different. Looking back, I can see that he was incorporating the key idea of this book: The secret to effective teaching is to connect with students and to actively involve them in learning.

There are two main reasons students don't do well in school: They don't get along well with others (which may include teachers) or they don't do their work. Helping students change involves helping them succeed in doing whatever they need to do to learn. Every situation calls for getting to know the students and what they can do and then figuring out what you can do to help them. This book helps you in the process.

I learned about classroom management from Rudolf Dreikurs and William Glasser. Dr. Dreikurs, a psychiatrist and the best-known student of Alfred Adler, specialized in working with teachers and parents. He would give a lecture, then invite teachers to come up and sit with him at the front of the classroom and share a problem. He would have a conversation with individual teachers, making suggestions regarding their specific situation. They would come back and share what happened during the next meeting. He was connecting with his students—in this case in-service teachers—and involving them in learning by helping them understand and make changes to what they could control—their own behavior.

Several years later I was very fortunate to participate in the workshops of William Glasser, founder of reality therapy and choice theory. Dr. Glasser, also a psychiatrist devoted to working with teachers and parents, was using a similar approach to Dreikers's. Their approaches became the model for my own classes with in-service teachers. Every week teachers would share a challenge they faced with their own classes and we would have a conversation about a small change they could make. At first, everyone would be reluctant to share. Teachers are supposed to be perfect, and no one wanted to admit that they weren't perfect. Eventually, one teacher would share a situation—a student who had given up, a math class where no one brought pencils, a power struggle with a difficult student—and we would come up with possible courses of action. Other teachers would follow and volunteer to talk about their situations. At the next class a week later, these teachers would share what they had done and how it had worked. There was no shame and no blame. Everyone worked to support one another.

After a few weeks, everyone began to realize that we were all in the same boat—that everyone was facing challenges. Everyone began to relax, to take the risk to share what they were dealing with, and to have conversations about simple actions they could take to improve their situations. They were often surprised to find that simple actions could solve problems. This book attempts to capture the spirit of those classes.

Through the years, the conversations began to coalesce into draft after draft of the book you now hold in your hands. This book encourages readers to think about their own situations and what they can do to help students succeed. If one thing doesn't work, maybe another will. The book presents strategies for how to be more effective, and encourages you to have conversations with yourself and others about where you can take a small risk to make a change. Often, a small risk is all that's needed. As a child, my bedroom wall had a sign saying: *Even a turtle doesn't get anywhere until it sticks out its neck.* Seeing that sign every day for years got across a key idea—I can stick my neck out a little bit and something good can happen.

Helping students be more successful is just as important for us as it is for the students—something I learned from another teacher. When one of my former teachers asked me how I was doing, I answered that I was surviving. He informed me that surviving was not enough—I needed to find a way to thrive. My purpose in writing this book is to help you thrive—not through telling you what to do but by helping you identify, think about, and put into practice small changes in attitude and behavior that will help you and your students succeed.

Telling teachers what to do seldom works to change them. Instead, teachers need alternatives—possibilities for small changes in behavior that can change a situation for the better. The difficulty in using many best practices is that they need to be tailored to fit each situation because each situation is different. Here you will find tools that will help you figure out what changes might work best in your situation and how you can apply them.

Applications of best practices are always individual, unique, and creative. We don't have to try to be unique or creative; this happens in the process of meeting the needs of each situation we face. In my own work as a counselor with students from kindergarten through high school, the key has always been getting to know the students and helping them come up with plans that fit them so well that they were willing to try them because they were tired of being in trouble or because they wanted to succeed. Sometimes they just needed someone to help them see that they were smarter and more capable than they thought. This approach isn't turning over control to the students; it's helping them accept responsibility by helping them understand that they are in control of their own behavior. Have no fear: As long as you are in control of your behavior, you won't lose control of the situation.

I've packed many strategies and procedures into these short chapters in order to invite you to keep reading until you find something that resonates with you—something that can help you with the challenges you're facing right now. Every reader will take away something different because everyone is facing different challenges. Make small changes and see what happens. Keep those that work and discard the rest. That's the message of the book. All the rest is the detail of figuring out how to do it.

Acknowledgments

This book could not have been written without my colleagues and students. In particular, thanks to all the MAE teacher interns, in-service teachers, and colleagues who read portions of the manuscript and used the material in its various versions in their classes, especially Penny Miller, Fred Taylor, Ray Boehmer, Edie Powers, Dave Bethel, Kay Mantia, and Barry Crook.

Thanks to William Glasser and the members of the William Glasser Institute. My thanks also to Rudolf Dreikurs, who taught me about group dynamics, social interest, parenting, and using psychology in the classroom. Heartfelt thanks to all the members of the American Society of Cybernetics, who have provided a multiverse of ideas, conversations, and community. In particular, the teaching, conversations, and written work of Heinz von Foerster, Herbert Brun, Humberto Maturana, and Ernst von Glasersfeld have deeply influenced me.

Many thanks to Truman State University for a sabbatical grant to work on this project. Special thanks to all the student assistants who helped with typing, editing, and research, including Adrienne Gerke, Shellie Mayes, Christi Meredith, Andrea Kohler, Joe Murchison, Sharity Nelson, and Melissa Stevenson. Special thanks to my colleagues who read various portions of the manuscript, including Sue Magruder, Joyce Ragland, Jack Lockhead, John Hoffman, Donna Rhinesmith, Wendy Miner, Jan Grow, Paul Martin, Jenny Web, and Sheila Thurman. Thanks to Loddie Krepps for editing and formatting the manuscript. Most of all, for having critiqued and edited all the versions of this manuscript, especially the final manuscript, for many valuable suggestions, and for unremitting encouragement, thanks to Dr. Suzanne Louise Martin.

Chapter One

Make Small Changes

"Effective teaching may be the hardest job there is."

—William Glasser

"First things first."

—Anonymous

Every time you connect with students and involve them in learning, you engage them in powerful ways that make it more likely that they will choose to do quality work and to learn. You can't force this choice, but you can make it more likely. This book shows you how, through small changes, to be a more effective teacher.

THE OVERALL PLAN

This is a practical handbook for all grade levels—K through 12—that focuses on strategies and procedures that can increase learning and achievement. There are no prescriptions here; you bring your expertise on the age group and subjects you teach. The strategies and procedures provide ways for you to evaluate where small changes can make a difference.

Each chapter focuses on a key strategy, and each chapter head and its subheads are an outline of how to put the strategy into practice. You can preview all the ideas by reading the chapter titles, heads, and subheads.

Chapter 1 begins with a theme that runs through the book: making small changes. Chapters 2–4 focus on connecting with students. Chapters 5 and 6 focus on planning. Chapters 7–14 focus on involving students in learning in ways that also help them connect with learning, with you, and with the class. At the end of each chapter, a section titled "A Scrap of Conversation" provides a personal comment on the material. A question-and-answer section (Q & A) follows, addressing issues about which the reader may have concerns. Finally, a short section titled "Additional Resources" provides one or more books, articles, or online sources that readers may find helpful.

Act, Observe, Reflect, Choose

Expertise—where does it come from? There is a saying that there is a big difference between thirty years of experience and one year of experience thirty times. Expertise is the ability to understand a situation in a deep way and to have a number of options for how to respond to it. Expertise doesn't exist beforehand; we develop expertise through experience where we act, observe what happens, reflect on how the situation has changed, and then make new choices. This is the reflective practitioner model (Schoen, 1984), and it forms the basis of the approach you will find throughout the book.

The reflective practitioner model stresses that the way to become a master practitioner is to engage in continuous learning that results from observing and reflecting on our actions and their consequences. The key to success is to become a detective continually becoming aware of the attitudes and behavior of others, our own attitudes and actions, and how these interact.

The cognitive-behavioral model (Dobson and Dozois, 2019; Ellis & MacLaren, 2005; McMullin, 1999; Ellis, 1975, 1977, 1978) is an approach to problem solving that stresses identifying and changing thoughts and behaviors that interfere with thinking and acting effectively. The work of William Glasser (1969, 1975, 1998a, 1998b, 1999, 2001, 2006) has been enormously helpful to me in working with teachers, students and parents as a psychologist in the public schools. I've also used Glasser's work, which has greatly influenced this book, in private practice.

Both the reflective practitioner and cognitive-behavioral paradigms emphasize making changes in thinking and acting based on observing and reflecting. These paradigms are used widely in education and are supported by research and the wisdom of practice. This book mostly refers to working with students, but the strategies presented can also be helpful in working with parents, administrators, and fellow teachers.

STRATEGIES PROVIDE DIRECTION; PROCEDURES SPECIFY ACTION

This is a book of strategies and procedures. Strategies point you in a direction; procedures provide concrete actions that, when repeated, allow teachers and students to automate lower-level activity, leaving room for higher-order thinking and action. In every lunchroom, students and teachers alike converse freely while using their forks and spoons without thinking. By adding to students' repertoire of procedures through practice, we free ourselves and our students to focus on learning.

Every chapter provides strategies and procedures that can help you reinforce or reframe your current way of connecting with students and helping them learn. Reframing is looking at a situation in a new way. Reframing is changing, in a deep way, the stories we tell ourselves about ourselves, others, and the world. How you look at teaching determines what changes you are willing to make. You have to convince yourself of the desirability of any change, no matter how small, before you will do it.

The cognitive-behavioral paradigm says that you can change your behavior or you can change how you view the situation. Both approaches can work, and we will look at them both. We reframe all the time, changing how we view situations to help us deal with those situations. We can help students reframe how they see situations to empower them to think and act more effectively.

The book provides alternative strategies, procedures, and ways of thinking, and leaves you to decide what to use and when. The themes that follow are threads that run through the book. They overlap and link together with the strategies found in the thirteen chapter titles.

THEME 1: MAKE SMALL CHANGES

The secret to increasing teaching effectiveness is to make small changes in what you think and do and get your students to make small changes in what they think and do. Take small risks. Like jumping off a diving board for the first time, taking a small risk is not hard, but you have to be determined. A poster that hung on my wall as a child showed a turtle withdrawn into its shell with the words: "Even a turtle doesn't get anywhere until it sticks out its neck."

Make Changes Small Enough to Eliminate Fear

Fear gets in the way of change. Fear engages resistance. Whether working with yourself or with your students, the way to eliminate fear is to make a change that is so small that it doesn't trigger the fear response and resulting resistance. In the course of this book, we will consider small changes you can make—including ways to encourage students to take on difficult tasks through small changes you can help them make.

Put First Things First

We always have time to do what is most important: to discover, through observing and reflecting, what is most important, and then to put first things first. The objection we are most likely to hear from teachers is: "I have no time. I can't add anything else to what I'm doing." Therefore, the goal needs to be to do fewer things. Even making a small change can be impossible unless we see a reason for the change. An objection to every idea for making changes is: How will I find the time to do this? Where can I fit it in? We never have time to do everything in any curriculum. There are always things that are left out or that we never get to. We will spend much of the rest of the book considering what the most important thing might be at any particular time. Who decides what things are first? *You* decide, because you are responsible for student learning.

THEME 2: CONNECT WITH STUDENTS AND INVOLVE THEM IN LEARNING

Connect with students (Chapters 1–3) and they will be more motivated to cooperate. Involve students in learning and they will be more likely to learn. A friend who grew up in a family where no one was educated, but who liked to read, grew up to become a community college English teacher. Her brothers, who had no interest in reading or school, never graduated from high school. She felt connected to school and learning. They didn't. Everything you do to get to know students and to involve them in learning helps you influence them in positive ways.

The theme of involving students runs through all the chapters. Have students actively use ideas and materials in order to understand them. As Jean Piaget put it, "to understand is to invent" (1973). We create understanding by interacting with the world, having conversations, reading, writing, and listening (Foerster, 2014; Foerster & Poerksen, 2002; Glasersfeld, 1995; Maturana & Varela, 1992). Even when students listen and understand, it is because they already have the vocabulary and prior knowledge they need to make sense of what they're hearing—and because they're interested. If we've learned one thing from the study of learning, it is that there is no passive transmission of knowledge (though it may often seem so when learning feels effortless).

THEME 3: DESIGN AND TEACH FROM BIG IDEAS AND KEY SKILLS

Your first job is to figure out what you need to do so that students increase their understanding of content by focusing on the big ideas and key skills they need to succeed at the next level—and to do well on high-stakes testing. What constitutes big ideas and key skills is not always clear.

Every state provides standards (or has adopted the Common Core), but you are the one who interprets these standards and decides which big ideas and key skills to emphasize so that students learn. Chapter 4, Design Learning Starting from the Big Ideas and Key Skills, focuses on identifying the standards that need to take priority. Chapter 5, Design Lessons Starting from the Big Content Ideas and Key Skills, focuses on designing backward from the big ideas and key skills that students need to know by the end of the year.

If you have high-stakes tests, you also have the problem of deciding how to prepare students. A real issue—and the one we will emphasize—is how to work with students who lack the prior knowledge and skills they need to succeed while also helping well-prepared students to thrive and learn. Improving skills and content knowledge, especially skills of verbal and written language, has the best chance of improving achievement and helping students do well on high-stakes tests.

THEME 4: TEACH PROCEDURES

Using procedures is a theme that runs through the book, with special emphasis in Chapter 8, Increase Learning by Teaching Procedures, on how to enable students to automate lower-level behaviors so that they can focus on higher-level behaviors. Automating skills and procedures is essential in taking on complex tasks and deep learning. Teachers sometimes resist teaching procedures because they believe that procedures make students less free, but the opposite is the case. You don't think about using a fork, and you use it perfectly—and you don't feel less free.

When small changes become procedures and then habits, their cumulative effect over time becomes huge. This happens so regularly that we don't even notice that our lives are made up of small learned behaviors that have become habits. These habits become the engines that allow us to do all the complex things we do in a day. Help students automate lower-level behaviors and you free students to pay attention and learn more effectively.

THEME 5: PRACTICE

Think of all subjects in school as requiring practice and you have a useful way of thinking about how to improve knowledge and skills. Figure out what students need to practice and you have begun planning (see Chapters 4 and 5) what you need to do to improve achievement. Chapter 6 deals with planning for practice; the remaining chapters deal with practice in one way or another, using a variety of strategies including scoring guides, team learning, conversation focused on big ideas, and direct instruction.

What Needs to Be Practiced

Most classes include students who do not have sufficient prior knowledge to do well. It doesn't matter why students don't have the prior knowledge they need (culture, poverty, exceptionalities, low English skills, students from all social classes who lack interaction with adults, etc.); our job is to provide practice that enables them to acquire the vocabulary, funds of knowledge, and skills they need to succeed.

In addition to learning through practice to read, write, listen, and speak, students need practice in key skills, including describing, explaining, analyzing, contrasting, organizing, and synthesizing. Even paying attention is learned. We expect students to come prepared with prior knowledge and skills, but if they do not, we need to figure out how to give them the practice they need.

Chapter 3 deals with helping students practice making choices. When students practice using scoring guides (see Chapter 6), they better understand how to produce quality work. Chapter 8, on learning procedures, shows how to involve students in practice that leads to more learning and more efficient learning. The chapters on using teams to give students practice (see Chapters 10, Use Teams to Increase Practice, and Chapter 11, Plan Projects that Use Teams) can help you to increase practice time for everyone. Chapter 12, Use Conversation to Increase Learning and Build Community, completes an emphasis running through the book on the importance of conversation as practice.

Direct instruction is a term for teacher-guided learning that includes demonstration, modeling, practice, and evaluation. Chapter 13, Involve Students in Your Presentations, presents ways of combining teacher presentations with student practice. This chapter brings together the themes of connecting, planning, and involving students to help you clarify your vision of how to bring many different techniques and approaches together.

Students Need to Use Key Skills to Understand Big Ideas

Usually, it's the teacher in front of the class who uses key skills like describing, explaining, and analyzing the big ideas. Throughout the book, the rationale for the use of scoring guides, practice, student products and performances, conversation, and other techniques is that it is the students who need to learn and practice key skills to understand and use big content ideas so that they will do well at the next level or grade and on standardized tests designed to measure their ability to understand and use key skills and big ideas.

THEME 6: ENCOURAGE STUDENTS AND YOURSELF

Every successful small change builds on strengths. Typically, teachers want to apply a new approach to their most difficult situations. Instead, build your confidence and your skill by first using strategies and procedures where they are most likely to succeed. Use them with students who are likely to cooperate; then, after you've had some success, move on to using them with more challenging students. Nothing works all the time, so start with the low-hanging fruit. Even if not all of your difficult students change, some will. Sometimes most will.

Go a Little Beyond Current Skills

The way to master any skill is to practice tasks that are a little beyond what we are currently capable of doing (Colvin, 2010). If students take on tasks a little beyond what they are doing currently, their skills will improve (Vygotsky, 1978).

Implement changes one at a time. Identify small changes and stick to making one change at a time. With your students, pick your battles—decide which behaviors you want to change—then have students practice behavior within their ability to accomplish tasks. Focus on changes that address your concerns.

Set Reasonable Expectations

The purpose of preparing is not to be perfect but to be able to recover when you do make a mistake. Teaching is always uncertain; every time we do something, it turns out a bit differently than it did the previous time. A friend who invented and fabricated large metal equipment offered an excellent piece of advice: Never set a pace you can't maintain. Whatever you do, be reasonable with yourself—and your students.

Expect that you will have success. Sometimes success can be instantaneous; sometimes it can take weeks or months. You already know that there are no magic bullets that work with every student every time in every situation. Success is not automatic or guaranteed. We all have difficult situations where the outcome is uncertain—situations where we have not yet been able to connect with certain students or involve them in learning. Sometimes (paraphrasing Harry Wong), the goal is to continue working for success with every student, even if you get to the last day of school and have not yet succeeded with everyone. There's always next year.

A SCRAP OF CONVERSATION

We figure things out through conversation. These paragraphs at the end of each chapter are one half of a conversation I wish I could have with you. You can start to learn anything from a book. This one is as accurate and honest as I could make it. However, the best way to learn the strategies and procedures in this book is through conferences and workshops. I've gone to many conferences of the William Glasser Institute—conferences that had us sharing, role-playing, and doing activities individually and in teams. I've also gone to conferences of the National Science Teachers Association—ten to fifteen thousand teachers from kindergarten through high school coming together to learn or to share exciting ways of involving students in learning. An inspiring time—and I'm not even a science teacher.

CONCLUSION

A small change in an attitude, a work habit, a learning strategy, a procedure for relieving stress, or even a small change in a schedule can make an important long-term difference when it becomes a habit. Whether we're working to deal with our challenges or attempting to help someone else, workable solutions come from three sources: (1) connecting with the person we're working with; (2) involving the other person in the challenge at hand; and (3) working on our thinking, feeling, and acting. When attitude, motivation, involvement, or work habits improve, learning improves. It doesn't have to be so, but often it is so.

Take a realistic approach; put your energy into doing what makes sense to you and is reasonable. Implement what makes sense to you. In the areas where what you're doing is working, continue as you are; don't fix what isn't broken. When you intervene, ask learners to consider changes they're ready to consider and then make those changes. Almost all teaching comes down to helping learners change specific behaviors. The more you learn about students, the more easily you can help them. This book provides strategies that will help you use your expertise and experience to generate alternatives for working with students that are *simple, doable, and measurable*, an idea found in Glasser's choice theory (Irby et. al., 2013, p. 486).

Q & A

Q. *I've skimmed through the book. There's no way I could put all these ideas into practice.*
A. Identify one idea and focus on that. You can still read the whole book and make notes about areas you might want to tweak in the future.

Q. *All my classes are heavy content classes—I always have a lot of material to cover.*
A. You have to make choices. Make choices in light of what will help students learn, retain, and apply skills and content needed to do well in future learning and on high-stakes assessments.

Q. *How can this book be aimed at both beginners and experienced teachers?*
A. The focus in the book is on paying attention to what you're doing, observing how it's working, and then reflecting on what you might do differently. Regardless of how experienced we are, we're always paying attention to what's working and what isn't—and reflecting on what we can do about it. Sometimes we stop doing something effective for no particular reason. When you find practices you are already doing, you will be reminded that you are already doing this and that it's working—and you should continue to do it.

ADDITIONAL RESOURCES

Esquith, R. (2007). *Teach like your hair's on fire: The methods and madness inside room 56*. New York, NY: Penguin Books.

An enjoyable read about a teacher's commitment to the power of small and simple things, like a classroom motto ("Be nice. Work hard."). Esquith emphasizes practical ways teachers can engage students regardless of background, difficulties, and challenges in learning. There are plenty of practical ideas and principles in this book that can help teachers make an extraordinary difference for the learners in their classrooms.

Chapter Two

Connect Through Getting to Know Students

"Seek first to understand, then to be understood."

—Steven Covey

"To understand a person, you must see with his eyes, hear with his ears, and feel with his heart."

—Alfred Adler

What is the best way to reach your students? The better you know your students, parents, and community, the better you can make good decisions about what will work. Get to know your students well enough that they feel you understand and like them. Learn their strengths, what they don't understand, and what they think, and you will learn what might help them.

When a high school student at a US Department of Defense school broke into tears during a social studies class, her teacher already knew that her father had just left for Iraq. The teacher reacted calmly and empathetically, allowing the student to leave the room to go to a counselor with a nod and a few words. You don't have to know all your students equally well. Ask the question: *How well do I know the students who don't do their work, don't get along with others, or have other problems?*

CONNECT WITH STUDENTS TO GET THEM INVOLVED

For most of us who have become teachers, learning in school was a competitive experience where we worked on our own and achieved on our own, regardless of how we felt about the teacher. Sure, we look back with fondness and respect on those teachers with whom we felt connected, but there were also many teachers we didn't feel connected with—and we still did our work. We still did our best because we felt connected to parents, friends, or extracurricular activities.

Many students will not work in school because they do not feel connected to school, do not have sufficient skills, or have given up. The better you get to know your students, the more likely you are to be able to help them develop a picture of school as a positive place, a place where they can succeed. For many students who do not have a mental picture of school as a positive, need-meeting experience, little can be done to induce them to learn (Glasser, 1998b).

Help Students Make Connections

It was only through my work as a psychologist working with students, their parents, and their teachers that I came to see that to reach those students who don't do well in school, don't like school, and resist making an effort to learn and do their work, understanding their culture and interests in school is essential for changing their attitude. Use examples and activities that relate to their worlds, and students can begin to feel connected. Help students improve their skills by thinking, writing about, and discussing what they know and understand (Bruner, 1960). There's no substitute for concrete experience, especially for those students who come to school with few experiences that connect to school learning (Bruner, 1961).

WAYS TO CONNECT WITH STUDENTS

There is no magic way to connect with students. Reading the following is a chance to review where you might make a small change. Remember that reading itself is a form of rehearsal—a way of thinking through what you're doing and what you might change.

Begin With the Intention of Getting to Know Your Students

Connecting means developing relationships. Jack Magruder, former president of A. T. Still University, president of Truman State University, science education professor, and high school chemistry teacher, came to my class of teacher interns to share what he had learned about being a successful teacher. The interns were eager to hear what he had to say. He talked about one thing—the importance of developing a relationship with students and their parents. Once he had students and their parents on his side, teaching chemistry and maintaining high standards was not a problem.

Having the intention to pay attention and listen—especially to students we find it difficult to connect with—organizes our perceiving, thinking, and decision making. If you're on the lookout for ways to get to know students, you'll find them.

Greet, Use Names, Pay Attention

Some teachers greet their students by name, or nod as they come in. That's for you to decide. If you're not doing it because you feel uncomfortable, consider that this narrows your opportunities to influence students. Do something that makes you feel uncomfortable (and that you would like to do and that is not dangerous) and you become more comfortable the more you do it.

Greet students, use names, nod, notice what they are wearing, notice expressions—all these things will help you get to know students. I remember counseling a high school student who wore a T-shirt with a skull. One day he came in with a plain T-shirt. I didn't say anything, but I noticed. Don't be too busy to pay attention. Whatever you do, pay attention and you will learn things that will be helpful.

Engage Students in Short Conversations

You don't often have time for long conversations with students, but you can talk with them as you walk down the hall, when you stand next to them while they are in line, as they come into class, as they leave class, and so on. Conversations are a key tool in getting to know students and other stakeholders. Make it a goal to have a conversation with every student and then monitor your implementation.

The simple intention to have a conversation, however brief, with every student is likely to be enough to bring it about. When you find yourself thinking about one or more students who are a problem or who don't seem to be doing well, ask: *What can I do to get to know this student better?* If you make the effort, something good may come of it. There are no guarantees that everything will immediately or magically get better. The guarantee is that if you don't, nothing will happen.

Avoid Questions That Students Interpret as Prying

If you ask a parental-type question, students immediately clam up, so focus on what interests them. Like adults, students like to talk about themselves and enjoy having others take an interest in them. Ask questions in positive or neutral situations, not when a student is in trouble. Once you're in a power struggle, you can't have a conversation. In working with students—almost always students who were in trouble and were very defensive—I usually began by asking, "What do you like to do for fun?" I can remember only two students over many years of asking who refused to answer.

Pick Up on Students' Vocabulary but Don't Try to Be One of Them

Learn the vocabulary your students use and learn what it means so you don't embarrass yourself. I don't even want to give examples because by the time you read this they'll be out of date. Don't be afraid to use their slang, as long as it's acceptable. On the other hand, don't try to be one of the students. Regardless of your age, as long as you act as who you are—a certified teacher with a college diploma—you're not going to have a problem with being friendly.

Make Small Talk

Small talk—even just a sentence—can serve the very important function of getting to know other people without taking risks, which is exactly what you need to do to get to know students who already feel defensive around teachers. Enjoy the interaction, have a good time, and feel free to smile. If you're not a natural extrovert, keep in mind that you don't have to feel comfortable to do this. Just do it, and the more you do it, the more comfortable you will become. If you aren't good at small talk, practice with the checkout clerks where you shop. It makes their day go faster and builds your skill.

Let Students Know What They Do Well

Spend time identifying students' strengths. Sometimes we get so focused on students' weaknesses that we forget their good points. As Rudolf Dreikurs liked to say, you can only build on strengths. More than general praise or rewards, specific praise lets students know what they are doing well and encourages them to do better (Martin, 1980). There is a cost—it takes a little extra effort to identify what students are doing well and to use specific statements. General praise like "Good job!" is not as effective as specific praise. Praise the product, the performance, or the action.

INVITE RESPONSES THAT LET YOU GET TO KNOW STUDENTS

A big emphasis throughout this book is on increasing students' skills and involvement. Getting them to write and speak about themselves builds their ability to think, their language skills, their confidence, and their connection with school.

Give a Written Prompt

Help students to connect their worlds to content. Use questions or assignments that invite your students to think and write about what interests them, scares them, or motivates them. For example, if you're teaching math, give an assignment that asks them where they or their parents use math outside school. Ask them to write about what's hard about whatever subject you're teaching—math, writing, history, science, health, social studies, or others.

Design activities, projects, and papers that require students to reveal something of their thinking process and their conceptual worlds—but don't ask for personal information. In general, it's fine if students offer personal information, but don't ask for it. Use content-related questions and activities that also allow you to get to know your students better.

Table 2.1 contains sample questions you can use as part of a class exercise. These questions can also work well in class conversations. Try out those that fit your situations. Even better, modify these questions or make up your own questions. The questions you create will be related to your situation. You don't need to grade responses. The left-hand column contains general questions and the right-hand column contains content questions that require research or recall.

Table 2.1. Sample Prompts

Sample General Questions	Sample Content-Related Questions
If you had lived during the Civil War who would you like to have been?	*History:* What were the causes of the American Civil War?
What would you do if you had a million dollars?	*Science:* If you could change the environment, what change would you want?
If you could live anywhere in the world, where would you live?	*Social Studies:* What is the best thing that could happen to you if you lived in Russia?
If you could be anyone, who would you most like to be? Why?	*Literature:* Which character from the story would you like to be? Why?
Where do you use math in your life?	*Math:* Make a list of 3–10 things you would like to buy and research how much they would cost. How much would you have to save every week to buy them all in a year?

LEARN ABOUT YOUR STUDENTS' NEIGHBORHOODS AND COMMUNITIES

Get to know your students' neighborhoods and communities, and you will gain more insight into those students. The more you learn, the more comfortable you are likely to feel with them. Sometimes getting to know your students' neighborhood can be a bit scary. I was apprehensive when I agreed to teach some of the strategies in this book to the staff at a local prison. I was not sure I could connect with the employees or the inmates. My practice was to talk in-depth with as many of the employees as I could—on their turf—doing their job in the prison. Some were teachers working with GED classes, some were guards, some were workers in the small prison hospital, and some were supervisors in food service, in the laundry, or in the industrial shops.

The door closed behind me, and I knew I was on my own as a guard pointed me in the direction of the school. As I visited and asked questions about what the staff liked, what they did not like, what problems they had, and what they did, I began to pick up some of the special language that every community has. I also visited with inmates and talked with them about their jobs, the prison, and how they got there. The more I toured, listened, and visited, the more comfortable I felt. As I began to design materials to fit the special needs of the group, I began to think: *This can work!* Table 2.2 can help you review how well you know the community, the school, and the students you are going to work with. Check off those you have already done and those you think would be worth doing.

Table 2.2. Get to Know Community, School, and Students Checklist

To Do	Have Done	Activity List
		Visit the neighborhoods where students live. Ask someone who knows the area to help you if you're not sure about safety issues.
		Visit and shop local stores, including food stores. Talk to the clerks and fellow shoppers.
		Eat at local restaurants, including fast-food restaurants and/or other places your students are likely to visit.
		Attend local sports events, especially those at your school.
		Attend local events such as fairs, pancake breakfasts, parades, or a Martin Luther King day activity. Talk to people while there.
		Watch TV programs and films your students watch. Listen to music they enjoy.
		Talk with students or parents when they are not at school. They may respond quite differently at Walmart, a mall, or a basketball game.

CONNECT THROUGH DEVELOPING A COMMUNITY

Every aspect of the learning environment either supports or discourages learners. Human beings are social animals and learning is a profoundly social activity. Even when learning takes place as a solitary activity, it almost always involves encouragement from others. Once you convince yourself of the importance of encouraging community, you can find many ways to do this.

Diane C. gave me a pencil on my first day in the sixth grade when I moved to a new community in the middle of the school year. I later learned that my teacher had primed the students in the class for my arrival. This is but a tiny example of building community, but the fact that I remember this small act of kindness many decades later shows the power of simple actions to create a positive learning environment. What if you had a way to have all the students in your classes help increase the achievement of everyone in the class through their acceptance, help, and support? Wouldn't it be worth a small effort to make this happen? When you enlist students to help everyone feel belonging, you expand your ability to influence all the students you work with.

Powerful Learning Experiences Involve Community

Regardless of where we have experienced belonging to a community, we know when we have had a powerful experience. For me, it was being part of a high school band for three years (I was a late starter). The elements of high expectations, high motivation, individual responsibility, strong work ethic, and public performances came about because band members cared and the band teacher cared and insisted on a high level of performance. We didn't always achieve it, but we always worked toward it.

I can't convince you of the importance of encouraging community, but you can convince yourself. The learning experiences we look back on with fondness are usually those that involved a sense that we belonged, a feeling of ownership and responsibility, caring about others, caring about a result, struggling to make things work, struggling to resolve conflict when things don't go well, and hard work (Chavis & Pretty, 1999; McMillan & Chavis, 1986).

Anything you can do to move in the direction of your fondest learning experiences is worth trying. Like the other higher primates, we are profoundly social animals. We exist in community (McMillan & Chavis, 1986). Even when our learning experiences are solitary, chances are that we are encouraged by others. The intention to move in the direction of making your classes learning communities can reshape how you see your classes. The pages you read here are useful only to the extent that they shape your intentions. Changing your intentions reframes how you perceive, think, and act.

Develop Community Through Belonging

Helping students feel belonging increases their willingness to cooperate and to act responsibly. William Glasser expressed this idea when he said that responsibility is the ability to give and receive love. Responsibility and cooperation flow from social interest, from concern for others, and from a feeling of belonging to a community. Create a sense of caring and being cared for, and you encourage responsible decision making and acting.

Students who rebel, who refuse to cooperate, or who withdraw are the students who are likely to feel that they do not belong, that no one likes them, and that they have little power to influence what happens to them. Such students may be coerced into conforming, but without increasing their feeling of belonging, they are unlikely to cooperate.

Students who misbehave but feel that they are still a part of the group are much more likely to take correction and to cooperate than those who feel that they are no longer a part of the group. Encouraging a feeling of belonging can best be accomplished by integrating everyone into the group. Especially in highly diverse groups, creating a sense of community involves everyone in learning to listen, respect, and work with others who are different from themselves. All the chapters in Part III (Chapters 7–14) can help you increase learning by involving students, and, in the process, build community and caring.

Spend Quality Time with Students

One of the best things you can do is to have conversations with your students about their interests in neutral situations. For example, you see a student in the grocery store and you have a pleasant conversation. Don't bring up the student's behavior; you're in a "no problem area" and what you want is a positive interaction in a neutral situation. Work to increase the positive "no problem area," because this builds positive relationships and increases the amount of goodwill you can draw on when there are problems to address.

Overprepare So That You Can Observe

One of the best ways to feel secure is to come prepared—or overprepared. When you come overprepared, you are better able to pay attention and figure out what students understand, what they don't, and why. The band director cannot listen to what the clarinets are doing if she is trying to sight-read the score. A fifth-grade language arts teacher cannot see what his students are doing if he is trying to find the page the assignment is on. A high school teacher who is thinking only about his lesson can't spot the student who feels discouraged or depressed by the way she walks into class.

A small change that works is to identify the student (or teacher, parent, etc.) you want to pay attention to. Take a brief moment to visualize yourself paying attention to that person before you walk into the classroom; your nonconscious mind will tend to do the rest for you.

Put aside everything else when you listen. Consider how you would feel if you went into the principal's office and she continued to write a memo while you were talking. If you wouldn't like it, then don't correct papers and listen at the same time.

Maintain a Supportive Environment in a Crisis

Sometimes you may find yourself in a crisis situation—perhaps a student's parent has just died, or a student has just been killed and the death is affecting the entire school. Maybe you find yourself working with a student who is using alcohol or other drugs or who is in trouble with the law. Perhaps you are working with a student facing a serious illness, who has been in a serious accident, or who has been raped. While no teacher is likely to experience all of these situations, everyone will experience some of them. The tendency in all of these situations is to dwell on such traumas, asking, "Why is this happening?" In these situations, you need to be calm, empathetic, and truthful. Textbox 2.1 provides a very brief list of things you should do or be prepared to do. The important thing is to prepare in advance.

> **TEXTBOX 2.1. BEING PREPARED FOR A CRISIS**
>
> - *Ask now for a copy of your school's crisis plan.* Your school almost certainly has a crisis plan that spells out appropriate responses for crisis situations. If it doesn't, suggest that a written crisis plan be created.
> - *Share information in an age-appropriate way.* What students (and others) imagine creates more anxiety than knowing what has happened.
> - *Listen.* Feelings of anxiety, disappointment, and grief are a natural part of dealing with a crisis situation. They are not psychological problems to be solved. Though they are not fun to experience, they are normal human feelings.
> - *Act calm and unafraid.* Don't overreact and try to fix a situation that cannot be fixed. If you are calm and unafraid, your presence will be reassuring. Even if you don't feel calm, you can act calm. Also, if you are not afraid of intense feelings (your own or those of your students), you can more easily be reassuring and encouraging.

Gather Student Feedback Through One-Minute Evaluations

One-minute writing gives you a chance to get feedback from students about what they like, what's working, what's not working, and what you could change (Angelo & Cross, 1993; Barkley, Cross, & Major, 2005). One-minute writing enables you to learn about what is meeting students' needs and what is not (Brookfield, 2006). Change the language to fit the grade, group, and subject matter, but keep it simple. Simple questions give learners the maximum freedom and often result in the most thoughtful responses. Here are some sample prompts for one-minute evaluations (pick one):

1. What did you like best about the assignment?
2. What did you learn from this assignment?
3. What was confusing about this assignment?
4. What part of the assignment was hardest for you?

Prepare yourself for frank answers, including things you may not like reading (Brookfield, 1995). Be prepared for surprises. You can also do this activity orally. The disadvantage to this approach is that when students are not anonymous they may be reluctant to be honest. Keep in mind that the purpose of writing is not to have students evaluate you but to have them reveal something about their own experiences (Brookfield, 1995, 2006). What they write tells you more about them than it does about you, and it's your decision how to use this information. Don't ask for personal information. If students do give personal information, maintain confidentiality.

Move Beyond Pressure

Sometimes teachers feel pressured by administrators to pressure students, which destroys their rapport with students—to the detriment of learning. A relaxed environment is important for learning. Anxiety and fear get in the way of learning and remembering. Do challenge students and hold them accountable. Don't pressure. You can only challenge them and hold them accountable if they feel connected to you and feel part of a community.

This and Also That

Sometimes you need to combine practices that seem to be opposites in order to be effective. Table 2.3 gives examples of two sides of connecting with students.

Table 2.3. Connecting with Students

It's Important To:	It's Also Important To:
Develop positive relationships.	Hold students accountable.
Be relaxed and have fun with students.	Challenge students to complete difficult tasks.
Be friendly and cheerful.	Be confident and in charge.
Find time to do the work required to get students involved.	Balance personal and professional obligations.

Table 2.4 gives examples of practices for involving students that at first seem like opposites, but need to both be put into practice.

Table 2.4. Involving Students in Learning

It's Important To:	It's Also Important To:
Break skills into small easy-to-practice chunks.	Have students work at a level they find challenging.
Give direction and provide structure.	Give all students choices where possible.
Allow multiple tries and revisions.	Hold students to deadlines and high standards.
Give students choices that connect with their culture, interests, and prior learning.	Make sure that choices also involve students in learning the big ideas and key skills over which students are tested.
Take small risks and make small changes.	Be willing to leave your comfort zone.

Students need to tackle challenging work and to become competent as a result of that work. The main thing is to be reasonable. We can't ignore student interests if we want them to learn; we can't ignore curricula if we want students to achieve. Ideally, we need to do both at the same time, and we need to do what works.

A SCRAP OF CONVERSATION

Connecting opens the door to change. Sometimes just believing in students and letting them know that you believe in them can be sufficient to bring change. This approach can help even older students. A colleague who taught biology at a community college had a student who wanted to go to vet school. The student was competent but was in danger of flunking out because of personal problems. The teacher continued to encourage her until she finished the class. Several years later the teacher received a Christmas card that said, "Thank you for believing in me—Jennifer." Several years after that she sent an invitation to her white coat ceremony for veterinary school.

All the K–12 students I worked with were in trouble either because they couldn't get along with their teacher or their schoolmates or because they weren't doing their work. My job was to help them cope and give them hope. One day a fifth-grade girl living with a single-parent alcoholic father came in to see me for a short weekly session. We were doing a learning game called "Stop, Relax, and Think" designed to help students make better choices—in her case, by not getting into fights. Toward the end of the session, she shared an insight: "I know some students who could really use this!" Connecting with her and involving her in learning allowed her to open herself to learning a new strategy and to making better choices. Her willingness to make things better also gave me hope.

CONCLUSION

Whatever we do to build a supportive school community, when combined with appropriate teaching methods, can improve learning and achievement. When we feel pressure to increase student achievement, we can easily feel that doing more to support community is taking away time from learning, but learning is dependent on attitude, on perseverance, on motivation, and on relationships—all things that increase when you build community. Taking time to build community can encourage achievement in ways that focusing solely on instruction cannot.

Get to know students better and you enhance your ability to design effective lessons and to influence them to try. A supportive environment is not just a good idea, it's necessary if we want learners to understand, remember, and engage in higher-order thinking and problem solving.

Q & A

Q. *I like the idea of building relationships with my students, but some of the things they deal with outside of school are so serious. How can I really be connected and supportive and keep them engaged in learning?*

A. Listen, listen, listen. You don't need to ask personal questions, but if students offer personal comments, just listen. Don't give advice; don't try to solve their problems. You can't. It's appropriate to refer students when they are dealing with issues that affect their learning and their lives but which you are not trained to deal with. It is, of course, always appropriate to report suspicions of abuse or neglect.

Q. *Conversation—when do we have time for it?*

A. You don't have to have deep conversations (and deep conversations can be very short) with everyone every day. Over the course of several months, you can find time to listen to many students. I don't say *all*, because some teachers have several hundred students in a week's time where others have twenty or fewer. But what is true of one student's understanding is often true of others'. If students are doing activities in groups, you can listen to them in the group and learn where they have misunderstandings.

Q. *I have too much to teach to even get through it all. How can I justify spending time getting to know students' interests?*

A. There are always students you may be able to motivate and help by getting to know them better. These are the students to focus on.

Q. *Won't it be more challenging to try to teach students who have been encouraged to develop a sense of community? I worry that I might not be able to control my classroom.*
A. The two big problems most teachers face are students who don't do their work (or don't try to do it correctly) and students who don't get along well with others. Developing a classroom as a learning community addresses both these issues. Students are more likely to care about doing their work and getting along with others when they feel a sense of belonging.

The research also shows that when students tutor one another, learning improves for both tutors and tutees—including the very high-achieving students. The point is that students who feel part of a learning community are more likely to do better than those who feel isolated. As for losing control, again, students who misbehave are more likely to be those who don't feel belonging with the rest of the class.

ADDITIONAL RESOURCES

Payne, R. (2005). *A framework for understanding poverty* (4th rev. ed.). Highlands, TX: Aha! Press.

A short, powerful introduction to understanding students who come from a culture of generational poverty. In particular, Payne focuses on how a culture of generational poverty differs from middle-class culture and what teachers can do about it. It's important, however, to realize that students from all backgrounds can have beliefs, attitudes, and behavior that interfere with learning.

Chapter Three

Connect Through Helping Students Make Choices

"Learning is a dance between teacher and student."

—Heinz von Foerster

All students at all levels—as well as all adults—make choices that don't work. With students, these choices almost always involve either getting along with others or getting schoolwork finished. When students make poor choices, you have two approaches available: You can try to control students' behavior or you can connect with them and help them make better choices. Try to control students through power and you lose your ability to influence them. Help them meet their needs, and you connect with them and help them increase their ability to self-regulate.

There are two primary ways to help students meet their needs: (1) Design your class so that students meet their needs for positive relationships and involvement in the process of learning, or (2) teach students how to self-regulate so they can meet their needs by making appropriate decisions and acting responsibly. The rest of this chapter focuses on ways to help students make better choices.

HELP STUDENTS MAKE CHOICES

While it's not our job to make students happy, it is our job to help them learn to make better choices—especially choices about getting along with others and doing their schoolwork. This means helping them become more self-regulating, including being aware of choices, making choices, self-monitoring, and self-evaluating. The language of choice theory and basic needs (Glasser,

1975, 1998b, 1999) provides a framework for helping students think about their choices. It shows how helping students make better choices can help them meet their needs so that they can experience school as a good place to be. The next several pages describe Glasser's choice theory, including his ideas on meeting basic needs.

Basic Needs: Survival, Belonging, Power, Fun, and Freedom

All human beings want to survive, to belong, to have power over their own actions and choices, to have fun, and to feel free. Through experience, each person builds up an album of mental pictures of ways to meet these needs. Knowing what these pictures are can help us understand students and why they act as they do—and can also help us connect with and influence them. The utility of Glasser's list of basic needs is that both adults and students know what the words *survival*, *belonging*, *power*, *fun*, and *freedom* mean to them. However, it is useful to provide a brief description of each of these five terms.

Survival

Human beings need to meet their basic physiological needs for safety, food, and shelter. Although not usually a major concern of teachers, student survival needs to take precedence over learning. Students who are hungry, sleep deprived, ill, depressed, or afraid will find it difficult to learn.

Belonging

Human beings are social animals who look to others to find belonging. Learners get their belonging from family, friends, significant others, and sometimes school. Learners want to feel that they are a part of the group; they want to be accepted by others. What students most often like about school, especially as they get older, is that their friends are there.

Learners also want belonging from their teachers (even in high school) and from their peers. I remember working very briefly with a third-grader who was so violent that he had broken a sixth-grader's arm with a metal bar. What impressed me was how much he wanted belonging and approval and how willing he was to work on tasks when he felt belonging with teachers and other students.

Power

Human beings need to feel in control of their own actions, to be competent, to achieve, and to be recognized. Learners need to be able to succeed in a task they are given. If they feel they cannot succeed, they tend to give up. On the other hand, if they can succeed, they may be willing to work hard.

Fun

Students need sufficient variety, satisfaction, and fun in their lives. When they fail to get it, they often become withdrawn and depressed. Fun, as used here, means the reward we get from learning and doing. When we master something, when we succeed at something, when we figure something out, when we use our skills, we enjoy ourselves. This doesn't mean the teacher should be an entertainer or try to make everything fun. If students are doing work that involves them in developing their competencies and making choices, they will experience both frustration and fun. Bob Pike (2003), a well-known trainer of adults in business, says that we learn in proportion to the amount of fun we have.

Freedom

Human beings like to feel free. When humans have little or no choice, they easily become despondent and passive. The opportunity to make a choice engages learners in a way nothing else can. Choices also give students a sense of power and control in the learning situation. Interestingly, if you give students tasks that are just a little beyond their current ability and give them the freedom to figure out how to meet the challenge, they are likely to put forth considerable effort to meet that challenge.

HOW TO APPLY BASIC NEEDS

Once you understand basic needs, you can begin to apply these ideas in your teaching.

Design Learning So That Students Can Meet Their Needs in School

Much of what we know about learning, especially behavioral learning, comes from the study of rat learning. What motivates the rats is meeting their need for survival—typically, the rats in learning studies have been starved down to two-thirds of their normal body weight. If they succeed in learning, they are rewarded with food.

Obviously, we can't make students' survival contingent on learning, but we can enable them to meet their other needs in the process of learning. We can't make students like school, but we can involve them in activities where they can succeed—and we know that humans tend to like what they can do well (and to do well what they like doing). We can't make students value learning, but we can involve them in activities that get them to experience the value of learning.

Help Students Feel Safe

If students don't feel they belong, if they are bullied, made fun of, or otherwise rejected, they are not likely to be good learners. If students feel continually sad, depressed, or never experience joy or fun in school, they are not likely to be good learners. If students feel pressured, they are not likely to be good learners. Connecting with students through listening and paying attention to them helps students feel that they do belong—a practice emphasized in Chapter 1 and in this chapter. Working with students in ways that enable them to connect with others while learning is also important; this is discussed in Chapters 11 and 12 on team learning and Chapter 13 on conversation as a way of increasing skills and practice.

Increase Belonging, Power, Fun, and Freedom

The basic needs are met when students connect with you and with their peers in the process of learning. Identify practices that meet several or even all of these needs simultaneously and you have a good way to motivate students. For example, one way of simultaneously meeting the needs for belonging, power, fun, and freedom is through using groups of two, three, or four students to actively process, practice, and review content and skills (covered in Chapters 11 and 12 on team learning). Ask yourself: *What can I do to increase student belonging, power, fun, and freedom that also involves students in learning?*

Each situation is different, and it often takes considerable thought and some experimentation to figure out what you can control and how to use what you can control. For example, you can try to make students put their names on their papers, but no matter how much you remind them, if you continue to read the papers and try to find out whose paper doesn't have a name, you won't succeed.

Control what you can control. You might leave papers without a name on a table uncorrected, then students have to take responsibility for looking through the pile, finding their paper, and putting their name on it if they want a grade. You might also provide training by having everyone put their name on their paper first, monitor to see if they've done so, and then give the assignment. There are lots of things you can do; the point is to do something that you can control.

Agree With Complaints That Are True

Often students complain that your tests are too hard or the work is too difficult, but in fact they're doing the work and mostly doing okay. Just because students are complaining doesn't make this a problem. Students' feelings are not concrete unacceptable consequences that we have caused; our dissatisfaction with student complaints is not an unacceptable consequence that the students have caused. Agree with them, that, yes, the tests are difficult—and move on.

Sometimes a parent complains and is unhappy with the amount of homework you have given, although it is in line with what other teachers give and with school policy regarding homework. Just because a parent is unhappy doesn't make it a problem; there is no unacceptable consequence for either the parent or their child. Agree that the school policy does call for homework (Martin, 1983).

Increase Agency and Self-Regulation

Help students meet their needs and you also teach them agency, that is, the sense that they are can make decisions, act, and take responsibility. Students who feel a sense of agency and are good at self-regulation tend to feel competent and successful in school (Brookfield, 1991; Browne & Keeley, 2014; Nosich, 2011). Students who meet their needs for belonging, power, fun, and freedom in school are more likely to keep working when frustrated (Glasser, 1975, 1999). There is no five-minute fix, but there are many things teachers can do at all levels to increase agency and self-regulation—traits connected with achievement.

Listening to students' problems can be a good way to help them accept responsibility for those problems—and this increases students' self-regulation skills. Asking students to fix problems they are creating can be another way to help students accept responsibility for those problems—and this can also increase students' self-regulation skills.

You have an obligation to work to get students' goodwill and cooperation, but when you don't get it, you also have the right and the responsibility to deal with them. What if students won't cooperate? The answer is that you can always offer them a structured choice; for example, "You can take the test or receive a zero. Your choice." If a student still refuses to cooperate, then you let the appropriate consequence take effect. While cooperation is ideal, if students refuse to cooperate, you have the right and the responsibility to do whatever you think necessary.

Even in this situation, however, by doing what you need to do in a calm, nonthreatening, and nonpunitive way, you are providing an opportunity for students to learn self-regulation by living with the consequences of their actions. Of all the key skills and ideas that are part of a curriculum, the skills that comprise self-regulation are the underpinning that makes it possible for students to pay attention and to persevere in learning difficult key skills and ideas.

Have Conversations About Basic Needs

Short conversations about students' mental pictures can create connections with individual students and with the class as a whole. Questions about basic needs can be very simple: What do you like to do for fun? Where do you feel powerful? Where do you feel belonging? Where do you feel free? (I don't ask about survival because that is generally beyond the scope of what happens in school.)

As a psychologist dealing with students in trouble who were feeling defensive, I always did two things. First, I made a deal with the student: "I will ask you some questions. If you don't want to answer, you don't have to. Deal?" Students always agreed because I gave them the power to refuse to answer (which they then never used). Second, I asked the students about their need for fun by saying, "Everyone has a need for fun. What do you like to do for fun?" The answer always allowed us to connect and provided both of us with insight.

Table 3.1 provides a template of the four basic needs with questions that you can use for conversations or ask students to fill in. Invite students to talk about where they meet their needs in school and what they could do to get more of what they want in school.

Table 3.1. How Could School Be a Better Place?

Basic Needs	At Present	What Would You Like to Have More Of?
Love and Belonging: Where do you feel belonging?		
Power: Where do you feel powerful?		
Fun: What you do like to do for fun?		
Freedom: Where do you feel free?		

With older students, you can share examples of answers and ask them to fill out the form. (Invite students to share them with you if they wish, but don't collect them.) Or you can modify the form to fit a particular course, for example, by asking what their goals are for a particular course. Let them know that what they write down is up to them—and that their answers won't be graded or even collected. Usually, with a group, I don't collect the answers unless students want to turn them in. I've done this activity both as a whole-group activity and as a one-on-one activity and have never found that students find it threatening because they are in control of what they say and this is an opportunity to think about how school could be better for them (Tishman, Perkins, & Jay, 1994).

Answering the questions in Table 3.1 is an example of self-evaluation. Self-evaluation is not giving yourself a grade; it's deciding if you're getting what you want and what you want more of. Self-evaluation is asking whether you are happy with what you're doing and with the results you're getting. By helping students discover what they want and how to get it, you're increasing agency and self-regulation.

HELP STUDENTS DEVELOP NEW MENTAL PICTURES

Few students (or adults for that matter) have enough mental pictures of how they can meet their needs—or what is possible for them to achieve. You can help students become aware of their choices by helping them develop new, positive mental pictures of people, relationships, and activities. Only then can they become goal oriented, because only then will they have a clear idea of what they want. This is true of all students, but particularly those who have fewer experiences outside their neighborhood, a lower fund of knowledge, or a smaller vocabulary than they need to do well in school. School is one place where they can increase these necessary skills and experiences.

Design and Encourage New Experiences

Build experiences into your lessons because experience is at the core of the ability to learn—and the ability to meet our needs as we develop. Think of everyone, teachers and students, as having an album of mental pictures. Some students come to school with a very large and varied album of pictures; other students, not so much. Students with large albums find it easier to think about, talk about, and write about the world they encounter in school.

New experiences generate new schemas and pictures. A new activity (e.g., planting a seed, learning about computers, taking piano lessons, writing a poem, or doing a science project) generates new experiences and new mental pictures. If learners do not continue to accommodate to new experiences, they lose their capacity to learn as their schoolwork becomes more complex.

Similarly, teachers with a wide variety of experiences may be flexible, see more possibilities for doing things, and feel more comfortable with encountering an ever-wider variety of situations in their schools. My colleague

Judson Martin had all the students in his educational psychology course complete an assignment that required them to try out new experiences, provided they were legal and safe. These future teachers wrote about how they were surprised when they tried a new food or visited a place they had never been. It encouraged them to stop avoiding new things. If they tried something they didn't like, they didn't have to repeat it. The point is that doing new things always involves us in learning and expanding our understanding of the world.

For all of us, teachers and students, a mental picture of what we want is the starting point of understanding something, wanting something, or going after something. And of course, we do not have a mental picture of something unless we have some experience of it. This is why it is so important to take children and adolescents on field trips to museums, businesses, concert halls, colleges, zoos, civic buildings, and so on, and then to talk about and discuss these experiences. This is also why it is so important that students have hands-on experience in school of making music and art, writing stories, and using computers, measuring sticks, and other tools. Firsthand experience also enables students to know what quality work is.

GLASSER'S APPROACH TO PROBLEM SOLVING

William Glasser created a method of problem solving (Glasser, 1975, 2001; Martin, 1983) that thousands of teachers have used to help students make better decisions by inviting them to think about what they can do to solve problems, including getting out of trouble. You can use Glasser's problem-solving procedure with a single student, a small group, or the whole class for situations like:

- Planning a trip
- Working on a project
- Doing a research paper
- Completing homework
- Addressing unacceptable behavior.

Note that only the last item in the list is a discipline situation. If you use the problem-solving steps only for unacceptable behavior, students will tend to see the steps as having to do with discipline and correction. If students are consistently guided through the procedure one step at a time in a nonjudgmental way, the procedure becomes part of their thinking. When they follow through, they increase their sense of agency and their self-regulation. They also meet their need to feel more free and more powerful because they're in charge of making decisions and following through on them.

There are many similar methods; Glasser's has the advantage that it requires only four easy-to-remember questions. The advantage to using the same questions every time (in addition to quickly memorizing them) is that students also learn the questions and can get better at using the method. Here are the four questions:

Question 1. *What do you want?*
This can also be phrased as:

- What is something you want?
- What is something you do not want?
- Who could give you what you want?
- How would you feel if you got what you want?

Question 2. *Is what you're doing working?*
Encourage students to focus on their behavior. Help students become aware of their power to make situations better or worse. Students already exercise power, but often without being aware that they are making a choice and that they are responsible for that choice. Here are some additional questions:

- Is what you're doing helping?
- Is what you're doing getting you what you want?

Closed questions that deal with specific situations can be useful. For example:

- Do you want to pass math enough to get a tutor and study more?
- Do you want to be a writer badly enough to be willing to write for ten years without recognition?
- Are you making the teacher a better or a worse teacher?

Question 3. *What can you do about it? When?*
Get students to brainstorm a simple, doable, measurable plan—and get them to pick a time when they will follow through on their plan. Questions you could ask include:

- What could you do to make the situation better?
- What are you going to do about it?

Be careful when accepting responsibility. Accepting responsibility for students' problems can have negative consequences, including:

- Discouraging students from accepting responsibility for their own problems
- Making it more difficult in the long run for students to cope with problems
- Increasing the probability that in your frustration you will use behavior such as nagging, moralizing, and preaching, that may damage your relationship with students (Gordon and Birch, 2003)

Question 4. *How did it work?*

Get students to commit to a time and place they will review with you how their plan worked.

Difficult Situations

When difficult situations arise, you need some strategies.

Listen Carefully

When you do not feel that you have to solve the problem, you can listen better because you are not trying to solve the problem in your head while a student is talking.

When something is not your problem, remind yourself, "This is not my problem."

You may be upset by the idea of not owning student problems, especially those that desperately need solutions. It is easy to make the irrational assumption that because we want desperately to help and because a solution is desperately needed, we can find a solution by owning the problem.

Feeling desperate results in poor judgment more often than it succeeds in helping. Listening and allowing students to consider their options (if they wish to do so) is a more realistic approach to helping than taking on students' problems. We cannot always solve others' problems, no matter how much we want to.

Avoid Defensiveness

Avoiding defensiveness is also a good way to avoid power struggles with parents, administrators, and other teachers. Friend and former colleague, Dr. Jack Ross, former high school English teacher, principal, superintendent, and professor of education, used to give me a hard time, always ending with a laugh and the words of advice: "Never be defensive." I eventually learned to follow it because of all the practice he gave me.

Think of feeling defensive as a form of cooperation. A student does something (intentionally or unintentionally) to threaten a teacher, and the teacher cooperates by feeling threatened. Teachers can learn to reduce their feelings of defensiveness by changing their expectations from "I have to be treated a certain way and students have to act a certain way" to "I prefer that students behave a certain way, but I will cope with whatever behavior comes up" (paragraph quoted from Martin, 1980, p. 132).

Avoid Demands for Agreement

Don't ask students to agree with your decisions or actions. A teacher friend of mine said that she wanted students to say, "I want to do it," because this relieved her of feelings of guilt. Make decisions, whether or not students agree. By insisting that students should agree, teachers invite a power struggle. This does not mean ignoring students' opinions but rather reminding yourself that students will not always agree that the teacher is right—and that's okay even though it feels uncomfortable.

Be Empathetic

When something is not your problem, don't take responsibility for solving that problem, but do be empathetic. Empathy means understanding how another person feels and understanding their hurt, anger, and frustration without being hurt, angry, or frustrated ourselves. When we start feeling hurt, angry, or frustrated ourselves, we easily start moralizing, giving advice, or otherwise trying to bring about a solution. Your understanding helps others respond more calmly even when no solution is forthcoming.

A SCRAP OF CONVERSATION

One day, while in a session using Candyland to evaluate a kindergartener for basic knowledge, willingness and ability to follow direction, ability to handle setbacks, and appropriate social skills, I realized that working with the kindergartener in front of me fit me better than being an administrator and attending a committee meeting with the dean—which was going on at that very moment on the other side of town.

Sometimes connecting with students involves participating in human suffering. As a psychologist doing counseling and evaluation, I was given students in trouble and then expected to fix them. The first task was to connect. Most of the students were poor, many had individualized education programs (IEPs), some were depressed, a few had been sexually abused, most didn't like school because they weren't succeeding. So many stories that can't be told here, but connecting allowed them to cope better.

CONCLUSION

At one time or another all students—and all adults—have trouble meeting their needs. Students who can't meet their needs for belonging, fun, freedom, or power in school do not find school satisfying and are not interested in learning things that have little interest or meaning for them. We need to plan learning that helps students meet their learning needs and their basic needs, even though we may feel we don't have time.

Q & A

Q. *What does helping students make good choices have to do with learning content? I'm not sure I have time for this!*
A. Self-regulation is not just about discipline. It can be a big problem for poor academic achievers. The procedures in this chapter are aimed at getting students to think and act in a more self-regulated way. These same procedures also can be used to help even motivated, high-achieving students to better plan and carry out their work.

Q. *Isn't self-evaluation the same as grading yourself?*
A. Self-evaluation, as William Glasser used the term, means having students ask questions about their thinking and acting, such as, "Am I getting what I want?" and "Are my actions helping me get what I want?" Students can be helped to decide if they want to do quality work and then be asked to evaluate what they need to do to make their work quality work. The questions are simply a process that students can use to evaluate their own (or anyone else's) behavior. You can adapt the ideas to fit your circumstances and needs.

ADDITIONAL RESOURCES

Glasser, W. (2006). *Every student can succeed.* Temecula, CA: Black Forest Press.

> Glasser's best ideas on connecting with students, eliminating failure, encouraging competence, and meeting basic needs.

Gordon, T., & Birch, N. (2003). *T.E.T.: Teacher effectiveness training.* New York, NY: Three Rivers Press.

> Still an excellent guide to classroom management. Gordon developed the "problem ownership" paradigm described in this chapter. Gordon and Birch are especially relevant to working with high school students, though their ideas can be used with students in the middle and upper elementary grades as well.

Chapter Four

Design Learning Starting From the Big Ideas and Key Skills

"Begin with the end in mind."

—Steven Covey

"I can't wait to get to school in the morning."

—Barry Crook, eighth-grade teacher

"I think education is both using and improving knowledge and that changes the whole picture."

—William Glasser

Chapter 3 dealt with connecting with students through getting to know them—which enables you to more easily involve them in learning. The remainder of the book focuses on connecting with students through involving them in learning. Learning is key. But what learning? The purpose of this chapter is to help you to plan backward from the big content ideas and key skills that students need to learn to succeed at the next grade or level and to do well on high-stakes testing. This chapter focuses on four things:

- awareness of the state standards (which may be the Common Core standards) that articulate the knowledge and skill students need to do well at the next level of learning and to do well on high-stakes testing,
- the need to prioritize standards so that you focus on the big ideas and key skills needed to reach state goals and to do well on high-stakes testing,
- the need to use the big ideas and key skills to modify the curriculum in the direction of meeting state goals and doing well on high-stakes testing, and

- the need to determine the prior knowledge and skills of your students and then to modify the curriculum in ways that will enable them to learn.

Addressing the four goals listed above is an extensive process that is best accomplished in groups at school or district workshops. However, even if you are working by yourself, awareness of the need to identify and prioritize standards and then to make whatever modifications are necessary to help students meet the standards that will be tested over can make you a more effective teacher. If you are already engaged in this process, the chapter will help you consolidate your efforts.

BACKGROUND CONSIDERATIONS

A big content idea is a network of concepts, facts, and applications that constitute an understanding of that big idea. A key skill is what the learner is expected to be able to do with a big content idea. To learn the big ideas, students need to be involved in using skills such as describing, explaining, comparing, organizing, applying, synthesizing, evaluating, making decisions, and other forms of practice (Anderson, 2001; Bruner, 1961; Dewey, 2007; Bloom, 1984).

A key skill (such as describing, explaining, etc.) may seem to be a general skill, but it is usually paired with particular content. We all know what describing means, but there is no general skill of describing. This is why deep understanding of content comes through an intensive development of skills used to understand content and intensive development of specific skills comes from immersion in content. This also explains why projects and activities that extend a bit beyond learners' knowledge are valuable: They develop interlocked skills and content. What is obvious in the study of mathematics—namely, that skills and content are interlocked—is true for deep learning of all subjects.

Standardized tests are typically tests of interlocked content and skills, which is why teaching to the test is usually of limited value. It's better to focus on developing the interlocked content and skills the tests assess—which means not focusing on the tests. The purpose of raising the issue of high-stakes tests in these chapters is not to encourage a focus on such tests but to clarify why "teaching to the test" doesn't usually work and may even be a waste of time because it doesn't prepare students well.

The Need for Prior Knowledge

Prior knowledge is important; in fact, it is one of the best predictors of ability to do well in a subject. To be able to succeed, students need to come with appropriate prior knowledge. Every teacher is familiar with students who may be able to decode the words on a page but who do not have the network of vocabulary, language skills, and specific content ideas they need to comprehend print materials, verbal presentations, or conversations. If we want students who lack necessary prior knowledge to succeed, we have to find out what prior knowledge students lack and then find ways to help them acquire that knowledge. One way to begin is to be on the lookout for such problems and to be alert for opportunities to address them.

Skills and Content Interlock

Successful practice builds skill through understanding content. Skills cannot be successfully practiced in isolation from content. Understanding the big ideas in all subjects is rooted in the successful practice of skills in connection with specific content.

We don't think of learning subjects in school as skill based because the skills being practiced are so taken for granted that they become invisible (except in mathematics, where skills and content are almost identical).

Textbooks tend to focus on presenting information, but information is only inert knowledge unless it is used—and using information involves skills. State standards and standardized tests incorporate information into a context where students need to do something with the information: analyze, describe, contrast, compare, decide what goes together, decide what doesn't fit. Unless students practice these skills, they won't meet the standards or do well on tests.

Learning from a lecture requires listening skills as well as a fund of information and experience that allow listeners to understand. Just as you need to know more than what you say when you give a presentation, students need to know more than what you say in order to understand what you are talking about.

The Need for Practice

While we all know the importance of practice, many of us also feel enormous pressure to cover material because it might be on a high-stakes assessment. "Covering material" doesn't work because students (and adults) don't remember information that is not tied to an understandable network of ideas. We as human beings literally cannot remember more than five to seven pieces of information that appear random to us. Tie information to a structure that makes sense, and we can understand and remember an almost unlimited amount of information.

Students can't learn skills separately from ideas—or ideas separately from skills. Both skills and ideas can be acquired and developed through practice. For example, the skill of describing can be learned in the process of describing big ideas. In the act of describing, students doing the describing are creating a deeper understanding of big ideas, as well as learning how to make descriptions.

Doing Well on High-Stakes Tests

Doing well on high-stakes assessments requires learning more than the answers on a particular test. Students who know facts but who don't have the big ideas and key skills won't be able to do well on high-stakes testing. Well-designed assessments always involve skills of reading comprehension, skills of mentally manipulating the ideas, and problem-solving and decision-making skills for choosing the right answer (Anderson, 2001; Bloom, 1984). Merely memorizing vocabulary, definitions, or facts is unlikely to help students do well because the student hasn't developed the skills needed to understand particular content.

PLANNING FOR TEACHING FROM BIG IDEAS AND KEY SKILLS

The method proposed here, from Wiggins and McTighe (2005), is to begin with what students need to know (the key skills and big ideas for each content area) and then use our knowledge of students to design lessons that increase those key skills and big ideas through practice. Practice includes anything students do that involves them in the skills of using, manipulating, applying, evaluating, and presenting the big ideas. This is a model that has been adopted by states and school systems, including the Missouri State Department of Elementary and Secondary Education Professional Learning Communities Project (2012).

Identifying the big ideas and key skills is important because most curricula and most state subject and grade-level standards identify hundreds of ideas and skills to be learned. Trying to teach hundreds of separate objectives individually doesn't work because students cannot remember or use large numbers of isolated facts. As a result, trying to teach hundreds of separate objectives doesn't lead to acceptable scores on high-stakes tests. Normed multiple-choice instruments don't typically test for discrete pieces of information. Instead, they measure students' ability to comprehend and make decisions about complex information—tasks that require skills of understanding and using big ideas. The solution is to identify the big content ideas and the key skills that meet state standards. In the process of involving students in learning the big ideas and key skills, students will, of necessity, also learn the subsidiary ideas and skills that go along with learning the big ideas and key skills. You are not discarding the subsidiary (or supporting) ideas and skills; these will come along in the process of focusing on the big ideas and key skills.

The steps that follow are a way to plan backward from what students need to learn in order to go to the next grade or level and to do well on whatever tests they are required to take. The goal is to prioritize what you need to focus on and to avoid just going through a curriculum, a book, or a set of books one step at a time without looking forward to where you need to be at the end of the process. The steps that follow can help you become more explicit about what you're trying to do.

Step 1. Identify Big Ideas and Key Skills

The first task is to make a list, preferably in the order they will be taught, of the big ideas and key skills that students need to know—and that they will be tested over. This can take a bit of detective work. A good place to start are your state standards or, if your state has adopted them, the Common Core standards (Council of Chief State School Officers, 2019). Some school districts even provide sessions for teachers to work together in small groups to examine their state standards and identify which standards are a priority. Your district may even have a name for the standards considered to be more important, such as *essential standards*, *power standards*, or *priority standards*. The important thing is that they are identified by the teachers who are doing the teaching, because only then will the chosen standards be part of their thinking and planning.

If the standards are not in the form of big ideas and key skills, transform them into the language that will enable you to think clearly about what students need to learn before they finish a class and go on to the next level. You can also go to the curriculum and look for the big ideas and key skills. Your curriculum is unlikely to prioritize its contents, so you need to decide where ideas and skills need to be emphasized.

If your students are involved in high-stakes testing, those tests can also be examined to see how district priorities line up with the tests. To do well, students need appropriate vocabulary and funds of knowledge as well as understanding of and experience using big ideas to think about issues and questions. Students need to be able to understand the questions and be able to think about which of the multiple-choice answers makes the best sense. This aspect of the test is the same every year. What is not the same, of course, are the actual questions, so learning facts or answers from previous tests is not going to work very well.

Your list will be tentative. As you become more explicit about what standards you need to prioritize, you will also become more aware of how your materials, activities, and assessments align with the standards. Working with a partner or a small group can help everyone become clearer about priorities, especially if you work in a group that includes teachers from the previous level and the following level. This helps everyone understand what students should have learned in the previous level and what they need in order to be effective learners in the following level.

Think of yourself as a coach whose goal is to prepare students for the next class and the big tests. The point is not just to generate a list of big ideas and key skills—someone could hand you the list on a sheet of paper—but to become more explicit about where the focus of your lesson plans needs to be. (Lesson plans are covered in the next chapter.)

Step 2. Create a Week-by-Week Overview

The second step is to break the semester or year into weeks and then decide how many weeks you can afford to give to each big idea and key skill. Preferably, use dates for the weeks so that you can see where you need to plan around vacations or special events. Whether you use a computer or pencil and paper, the physical act of plugging the big ideas and key skills into a schedule for the semester (or the year) will help you think about how teaching big ideas and key skills is going to play out.

One thing you will become aware of is that when you focus on your priorities, you will have to choose what will be given less time. You may be frustrated that you won't have enough time to spend on even the most important ideas. Nevertheless, you will begin to come up with a plan that will put first things first, allowing students to gain more over the semester or year than they otherwise would.

The first time you go through the process of scheduling how much time each big idea and key skill will receive, your plan may be very approximate. In practice, it won't work out quite as you planned, but that's okay because what you are learning from the planning process is more important than the plan you develop. Don't worry—you will be able to make changes as you move through the year.

The thing to avoid is going from one lesson plan to the next, covering what's in the book or the curriculum one step at a time. Without an overview of what students are going to be responsible for knowing and doing—and therefore, what they need to be practicing—your lesson plans will lack focus on the goal of involving students in all the key standards they need to meet by the end of the semester or year. The benefit of making and then reviewing a large-scale plan is that you clarify your thinking about how to best use class time. You will develop a new level of understanding and clarity that will increase your ability to do a better job of designing learning.

Since you can't do everything in depth, make choices based on making the key skills and ideas your priority. This doesn't mean you eliminate objectives from the curriculum; it means you can group smaller objectives into clusters around the big ideas and key skills. As for end-of-the-year standardized testing, tests attempt to measure skills and understanding; your students will do as well as they are capable of because you have focused on skills and understanding.

We always have time to teach key skills and ideas, but only if we come to grips with the reality that sometimes we may have time *only* for those key skills and ideas—though it will also be true that students will pick up subsidiary ideas and skills in the process.

Be as Detailed as Needed

Making a plan involves you in processing the curriculum so that you develop a clear understanding of what you're trying to teach. Some teachers are detail oriented and are not happy unless they produce a highly detailed plan of what they're going to do. Some teachers are big-picture people and are happiest when they identify the broad outlines of what they need to do, leaving the specific details until the week or even the night before. The more you work with a large-scale plan, the clearer your individual lesson plans (covered in the next chapter) will become.

Once you have an overview, you are ready to begin filling in the details—or you can save that for lesson and unit plans. Different teachers are going to have different amounts of detail. Work with whatever level of detail makes sense to you. If you find yourself revising how many weeks you will devote to a topic, that's fine. The details are going to change—you know that already. The point is that getting down at least some of the details helps you clarify your thinking.

Build in Slippage

In doing long-term planning, leave ten percent of your time open to handle delays such as unexpected absences, students having difficulty in mastering material, activities that take longer than expected, or overoptimism on your part. You may want to do this by leaving a day or more at the end of each major unit.

Revise Plans as Needed

Your large-scale plan is a work in progress. Revise it as often as you need to throughout the year. The important thing to keep in mind is that by repeatedly working with your large-scale plan, you clarify how to break the semester or the year down into units, weeks, and days. In the long run, creating a large-scale plan will save you time and allow you to better design the learning. You will ensure that you cover the most important content and the key skills and that you won't reach the end of the year (or the semester) with important chunks of content and skills untouched.

Step 3. Develop a Vision for What Your Class Will Be Like

To create a vision, first determine the need—and you've already done that with steps 1 and 2. Now you get to decide how you want to involve students in learning big ideas and key skills. Keep in mind that in focusing on big ideas and key skills, students will be picking up other knowledge and skills because big ideas always include rich networks of ideas and facts, examples, and applications.

We're not creating a product (an unfortunate term that sometimes creeps into education). We are involving students in deep learning so that they can do well in the future. While there might seem to be little or no time for projects, practice, and creativity, if these involve students in deep learning of big ideas and key skills, they are more than worth the time involved.

You became a teacher because at least some of the things you did in school were deeply rewarding, often because you worked harder and learned more and felt more satisfied than you thought you could. The legitimacy of those experiences comes from their value to you as a human being—and their success in involving you in deep learning of both content and skills. Skills don't come mostly from drill, they come mostly from being stretched beyond your present skill level.

We want to find ways to get students to stretch a little beyond their present skill level, and this comes from having students do things that are not easy. However, students won't become involved in doing things that are not easy unless they can feel involved. You can see amazing learning going on in early grades where students are creating their own books and in high school science labs where students are doing college-level work.

Students' interests and district, state, or national goals may not seem to have much in common, but you can design lessons that both develop student interests and focus on key skills and big ideas. You motivate students by involving them in activities and projects that they find challenging and fun. Using your knowledge of the key skills and big ideas, your knowledge of your students, and your willingness to take small risks, you can find ways to accommodate the needs of your students—and design projects, activities, and assignments that you would like to have your classes doing. Your creativity, skill, intelligence, and knowledge of the students all enter into the process.

Dream Projects

We all have a choice: We can move toward realizing our dreams of what we would like to have students doing or we can give up. We maintain our excitement as teachers by having a vision that excites us, and then putting that vision into practice by making small changes over time. Implement your vision in a way that always incorporates the big ideas and key skills students need to succeed. More on dream projects in Chapter Eleven.

A SCRAP OF CONVERSATION

Two teachers from the Northeast Missouri Regional Professional Development Center came into my classroom of undergraduate teacher education students, plunked down sets of state standards, put students in groups by grade and subject area, and asked the groups to go through the standards and pick out the big ideas and key skills. The groups combed through countless standards and reported back on their findings at the end of the hour. They weren't sure they had gotten it right, but that's part of the process. No one is ever sure they get it right, but it helps direct planning. As the saying goes: The plan is nothing; planning is everything.

CONCLUSION

As students, we use key skills to think; we develop key skills through immersing ourselves in content.

Begin by going through the state standards for your class and identifying the big ideas and key skills. If you're doing this in your school in groups (or have already done it), hurrah for you! Now plan backward from where students need to be at the end of the year and you have a recipe for helping students to do well, including on high-stakes testing. Even where we already have a curriculum in place, we have to find a way to make it work. If the curriculum is not written in terms of key skills and ideas, they are still there, hidden within the curriculum.

In any case, existing objectives, curricula, and even lesson plans can provide guidelines for what to teach. They can provide scope and sequence for your teaching. But they do not do the work of translating scope and sequence into an experience that results in learning. You have to do that; or rather, you *get* to do that. Identifying what ideas and skills need to take priority before dealing with lesson plans is putting first things first. The next step after doing an overview for the semester or year is to create a set of lesson plans, which is taken up in the next chapter.

Q & A

Q. *I don't have time now to cover everything. If I spend more time having students practice skills, I'm going to have even less time to cover things. How's this going to work?*
A. This is the dilemma all teachers face at all levels, from kindergarten through college. Building skills requires covering less material but can lead to greater achievement. Ask yourself whether your goal is to cover everything or to maximize the total amount of achievement in your class.

Research suggests that US schools tend to err on the side of too much breadth and not enough depth, resulting in low scores on standardized instruments used to compare achievement in different countries. So, the answer to the question, *"How's this going to work?"* is that you're probably going to have to go outside your comfort zone if you want to focus on key skills and big ideas.

Q. *Aren't you advocating teaching to the test?*
A. The idea of "teaching to the test" assumes that students can do well on specific tests simply by learning a body of facts. Most state and national tests require both general reading skills and specific understanding of content and the ability to choose among similar alternatives in order to do well. Teaching a body of facts will not help students do well because students are expected to understand the underlying big ideas that unite a body of facts and the key skills that involve explaining, analyzing, and comparing big ideas in terms of a body of facts. Put another way, it's simply more effective to use of your time to develop understanding of big ideas and the network of facts and ideas that make up the big ideas and specific content skills.

ADDITIONAL RESOURCES

Ainsworth, L. (2017, April 6). Priority standards: The power of focus. https://www.larryainsworth.com/blog/priority-standards-the-power-of-focus/

This free download does an excellent job of explaining the idea of priority standards, why they are important, and how to use them. Suggested by Sheila Thurman, consultant at the Northeast Missouri Regional Professional Development Center.

McTighe, J., & Wiggins, G. (2012). *Understanding by design framework*. Alexandria, VA: ASCD. https://www.ascd.org/ASCD/pdf/siteASCD/publications/UbD_WhitePaper0312.pdf

This free thirteen-page synopsis of backward design expands on the basics discussed in this chapter.

Chapter Five

Design Lessons Starting From the Big Content Ideas and Key Skills

"When I'm not prepared, I dread going to work."

—Barry Crook

"If you want to feel secure, do what you already know how to do. If you want to be a true professional & continue to grow . . . go to the cutting edge of your competence, which means a temporary loss of security. So, whenever you don't quite know what you're doing, know that you are growing."

—Madeline Hunter

Instead of thinking of lesson plans as a dreaded activity you have to do to satisfy administrators, consider lesson plans as an opportunity to design learning. Planning is an opportunity to increase your choices, your focus, and your control over what you're doing—and, as a result, to feel more free and less stressed. Chapter 4 focused on planning backward from the priority standards containing the big ideas and key skills that students need. This chapter focuses on the lesson plans needed to translate this overall plan into specific actions for each lesson and on making lesson plans simply and quickly.

Lesson Plans: Designs for Learning and a Set of Cues

Think of a lesson plan as a design for learning and as a set of reminders that cue the teacher to carry out the design. Once you identify the big ideas and key skills students need to learn, you can design how you will involve them in learning. A big idea cannot be contained in a sentence to be memorized. Big ideas are not big ideas unless they incorporate the network of ideas, facts, and applications that gives them meaning.

Baseball is a game that involves hitting a hardball with a bat and running around bases, but if you don't already know how baseball is played, this description, however accurate, won't mean much to you. To be able to understand and use big ideas, students have to practice using them. This means being able to listen, talk about, read about, and write about them. This is not teaching to the test but teaching to the standards—to the ideas and skills students need to do well when they take the tests.

DESIGN UNITS OR SETS OF LESSONS TO TEACH BIG IDEAS AND KEY SKILLS

Once you have an overview (from the previous chapter) that divides the year into the number of weeks you can spend on each big idea and/or key skill, you have a good way to plan groups of lessons.

An effective lesson is most likely to come from developing a simple, even obvious idea around which everything else—including facts—is organized. Be clear about what you want students to learn and what you want students to do to learn, and you have the basis of a lesson plan. If you can't say what the focus of the lesson is, how can you expect your students to get it?

We learn what we do. Teachers may see involving students in activities as optional—if there's time—because they don't understand that students don't learn big ideas just from hearing about them or reading about them but from manipulating the ideas. This is especially true for students who need to build up their language skills, their vocabulary, and their fund of knowledge. In particular, students—and also adults—learn best when they do tasks normally done by teachers, tasks such as answering questions, asking questions, summarizing, evaluating, using scoring guides, tutoring, and so on. (These topics will be discussed in future chapters.) Students don't need to do all these things all the time; at any one time they need to be doing some of them.

Trying to do too many things creates confusion. It is better to do a short presentation and one activity and then have students talk or write about what they learned. Avoid doing two or three activities with no chance for students to process what they learned or make connections with what they already know.

Design Lessons for Effective Practice

Students learn what they do, not what the teacher does. Doing well as a learner is a matter of long-term effective practice, not innate talent (Colvin, 2010) and effective practice can help students with low skills improve

(Payne, 2005). Later chapters focus on how to provide practice that helps students who need practice most and also enables good students to improve.

The goal in using activities and projects is both to involve students in ways that provide opportunities for practice and to encourage them to take ownership of the learning process so they will make the effort needed to learn. Your most powerful allies in involving students can be your love of your teaching area, the fun of working with students, and the ownership of learning that comes when students feel fully involved.

Design for Students' Prior Knowledge

Prior knowledge is an excellent predictor of how well students will do in a class. Students without an appropriate vocabulary and fund of knowledge don't understand a text even when they are good readers. For example, research shows that students who are poor readers but who understand baseball are better than good readers with no knowledge of baseball at reading and interpreting materials on baseball (Wexler, 2019). This means that prior knowledge is essential for learning.

Where do your students lack prior knowledge that they need to do well in your class? Once you figure this out, you can design activities that can help them better understand what they need to do and how to do it.

Design So That All Students Understand Instructions

Build in enough cues and detailed instructions to bring along students with insufficient experience in understanding and following instructions. Some students—including those with low English language skills—need more specific cues and instructions to be successful. Stepping students through instructions and procedures one step at a time (see Chapter 8) will help those with low English language skills without slowing down others.

Design for Self-Regulation Skills

Self-regulation allows students to pay attention to tasks (including listening), manage frustration, and persevere until tasks are completed. When we talk about self-regulation, we are not talking only about behavior problems. Learning is a self-regulated activity that is best accomplished when students know how to use specific strategies and know-how to monitor their use of those strategies.

You don't need to find extra time to work on self-regulation as a separate skill. The chapters on scoring guides, procedures, practice, and team learning provide ways of processing material and practicing skills that also teach self-regulation.

Limit the Number of Big Ideas to One Per Lesson

Designing lessons calls for courage. Sometimes the only way to involve students in practice may be to cut something—and that's uncomfortable. Even adults have trouble making sense of presentations, readings, or materials that don't have a main idea to which everything relates. You can incorporate examples, facts, demonstrations, and subsidiary ideas as long as they relate to a big idea.

Automate as Many Elements as Possible

Go to a well prepared workshop that a presenter has done dozens and dozens of times and you experience an energetic and effortless flow of presentation and activity. You're following directions, but you don't feel like you're being controlled. This comes from the leader developing procedures and then using them every time all the time. You teach the same material only once or twice a year, but you have the opportunity to develop procedures you can use every day or every Friday or . . . whatever you decide.

Some of these procedures don't even have to be put into your lesson, such as greeting students as they come in every day, putting a phrase for a key idea on the board, having students take out a pencil to do a short activity, giving a quiz on Fridays, and so on. Anything that you can automate, though it may take an effort to choose and then practice, frees up time and allows you to focus on what is happening and allows you to flow through the lesson in a relaxed way. This will be discussed in more depth in Chapter 8, *Increase Learning by Teaching Procedures*.

PLAN LESSONS AND UNITS USING A TEMPLATE

How can you find the time it takes to plan lessons? Consider planning lessons using a template. Any time you can partially automate an activity by turning it into a procedure, you make completion of the activity easier and faster—and free yourself up for higher-order thinking. To get ideas, look online. Simply type "lesson plan template" into your browser. Many templates assume that your lesson should be organized in a specific way and should include specific things you don't want—so you may want to develop your own template.

Table 5.1 provides a simple, easy-to-use template. The template allows you to divide each lesson into activities of your choice. An activity might be a teacher presentation, student practice, project work time, independent practice, group practice, and so on. There is no assumption about what you should be doing. That's for you to decide. The only expectation is that it is a good idea to estimate the amount of time each activity will take (more on this below).

Try the Table 5.1 template (you are free to reproduce it or modify it as you see fit). A paper version allows you to revise, doodle, and scratch things out—all part of the fooling around that is crucial to any design process—and you can make notes on it while in class. If you decide to use paper templates, run off as many as you need and fill them in as you go along.

Table 5.1. Template for Lesson Plans

Unit _____   Lesson Plan for _____

Date _____

Big Ideas _____

Key Skill(s) _____

Product or Performance _____

Clock Time	Time Blocks (# of minutes)	Activities	Materials & Comments

Time Blocks

The lesson plan template (Table 5.1) focuses on three tasks: Identify the big idea and key skill(s) for the lesson, divide the lesson into blocks, and then estimate how long each block should be.

Look at the next lesson or set of lessons you will teach. For each lesson, divide the lesson into blocks of time by activity, designating a time amount for each block. Activities include anything that takes time: transitions, giving instructions, distributing handouts or materials, dividing into groups, doing a task, cleaning up materials, handing in assignments, and so on. Be explicit about time units. When you give the lesson you will be able to notice how the short activities, instructions, and transitions went and where you can tighten up your lessons and become ever more expert at using your time well.

HAVE A "PLAN B"

No matter how much you plan, you cannot completely control what happens. You might plan to do an activity outside and it rains. You might plan an activity that you expect to take twenty minutes and students are done in ten. You might plan an activity that you expect to take ten minutes and it takes twenty minutes. (If it was a productive twenty minutes, congratulate yourself—you've found something that works.) Or you might plan to use technology and the computer doesn't work, the internet goes down, or the Smart Board quits working. Take home message: Make a backup plan—a "Plan B"—in advance so you won't be caught short.

Having a Plan B gives you a sense of security and control; you know what you'll do if Plan A does not work out. What causes the feeling of losing control is not that things don't go according to plan, but that you don't anticipate that things might go wrong and you don't have a backup plan.

Evaluate and Revise

Make a note of anything that needs to be changed on the lesson plan during and/or after you have taught a lesson—and make sure you do it the same day so you don't forget. Review the blocks and revise to better allocate time. The goal is to put yourself through a process where you observe, reflect, and then modify the lesson plan. If you do this regularly, you, like Sherlock Holmes, will become more aware of what is happening around you.

If you write more detailed lesson plans, after several years you will have trained yourself to think in terms of time blocks and student involvement, and your written lesson plans will be shorter because you will know precisely how to proceed through a set of activities. Spend more time designing lessons and noting revisions, and your lesson plans will become easier to make, and shorter over time.

A SCRAP OF CONVERSATION

I had to learn the hard way that teaching from one day to the next is more work and more stress than deciding upfront how much time is needed to be devoted to each skill and topic—and then making an overall plan for the semester on computer, and then making individual lessons plans on a template the week or even the night before in order to take into account what happened in the previous week or day. Create a rough plan for the coming year—or the rest of this year. The goal is to increase your expertise through planning, executing, observing, reflecting, and then deciding what is missing and what might work better. Your growing confidence will make you more relaxed and effective.

CONCLUSION

Plan for the semester or the year by creating an overview in which you divide the semester or year into weeks and then determine how many weeks you can devote to each of the big ideas and key skills that students need. Once you have this overview, use lesson plans to convert your overview plan into concrete lessons.

Use a template of your choosing (a calendar, list, table, or chart) that shows the activities for each lesson and how long each activity will take. Over time, lesson planning will become faster and more focused. Like a coach, observe how students are doing and make notes on your lesson plan so that you can implement your insights.

Q & A

Q. *How do I use the ideas for designing learning when the scope and sequence I cover is mandated by my curriculum?*

A. All the ideas in this book assume that everyone has a scope and sequence to follow. At the end of the year, we're responsible for what students learned. If what you're doing in a particular content area is working, there may be no reason to change. Sometimes we feel like it's our job to "cover" all the material, but it would be more accurate to say that we are responsible for finding ways to get students to learn the material.

Scope and sequence can always be viewed in terms of the big ideas and key skills that are contained within any scope and sequence. It's easy to get bogged down in trying to cover everything in the scope and sequence; the big idea is to identify the big ideas and key skills embedded in your scope and sequence and then to focus on those. You're still using the curriculum and the texts you are expected to use; you are simply being more careful about what you emphasize.

ADDITIONAL RESOURCES

Cawelti, G. (Ed.). (2004). *Handbook of research on improving student achievement* (3rd ed.). Alexandria, VA: Educational Research Service.

The most readable, friendly, and usable book on effective K–12 teaching methods and learning practices across the content areas; includes all the best practices that research has shown to be effective. Everything in this very complete book is supported by extensive research. It presents information on content area methods that you need in a format you can use. In an hour you can identify all the methods that lead to achievement in the subjects you teach at the level you teach.

Greeley, K. (2001). *"Why fly that way?" Linking community and academic achievement.* New York, NY: Teachers College Press.

An inspiring book-length example of a teacher using a community of learners to focus on the key skills and big ideas at the upper elementary school level.

Wiggins, G. (2012). *What is understanding by design?* [Video]. YouTube. https://www.youtube.com/watch?v=WsDgfC3SjhM
Wiggins, G. (2013a). *Understanding by design (1 of 2)* [Video]. YouTube. https://www.youtube.com/watch?v=4isSHf3SBuQ
Wiggins, G. (2013b). *Understanding by design (2 of 2)* [Video]. YouTube. https://www.youtube.com/watch?v=vgNODvvsgxM

An easy way to become more familiar with Wiggins's ideas is to view the online videos (Wiggins, 2012, 2013a, 2013b) designed to get teachers beyond teaching content and to consider what students need to be able to do with the ideas and skills they learn.

Chapter Six

Use Scoring Guides to Increase Quality Work

"No human being will work hard at anything unless they believe that they are working for competence."

—William Glasser

Why use scoring guides? Scoring guides are a flexible way to incorporate criteria based on big ideas and key skills in a way that can be understood and used by teachers, students, and parents. It can take a bit of work to create a set of scoring guides, but they give you a way to make expectations clear.

The previous chapter focused on planning backward to include all the big ideas and key skills students need to be prepared for the next grade or class and to do well on high-stakes testing. Scoring guides are a way to clarify what students need to learn and demonstrate. This chapter focuses on making expectations concrete by incorporating criteria relating to big ideas and key skills into scoring guides.

WHY USE SCORING GUIDES?

Making scoring guides requires an initial investment of time, but it saves you time grading and increases the quality of student work. Once you have made an effective scoring guide, using it gives you a detailed picture of what students are learning and helps you to revise lesson plans and your overall plan.

If only the teacher uses the scoring guide, it may improve evaluation but it doesn't necessarily improve learning. The real power of using scoring guides comes from having students use scoring guides to evaluate examples and their own work, especially if they are allowed to revise their work.

Increasing Student Control Over Quality and Achievement

We can't measure learning directly; we can evaluate students' products and performances. Scoring guides make evaluation more transparent, give students more control, increase student investment in learning, and reduce student anxiety and the "don't look back" approach to getting back graded tests and assignments. Students often have little idea of why they scored as they did or what they can do about it. What constitutes a quality product or performance has to be learned, and scoring guides provide a way to learn.

When students get a grade, they know when their work is not high quality, but they may not understand what they need to do to improve. Scoring guides help students learn what constitutes quality for a specific product or performance.

Scoring Guides Improve Evaluation and Grading

Scoring guides allow you to grade products and performances in a systematic and defensible way you can explain to students, parents, and administrators. Scoring guides let students know what they did well and where they can improve (Angelo & Cross, 1993; Gronlund & Waugh, 2009).

Scoring guides can help teachers avoid the false issue of "subjective versus objective" grading. The teacher's judgment will be considered reasonable when students and parents understand the judgment and have also been using the same criteria. Scoring guides can also cut your grading time for projects, assignments, and even exams where higher-order thinking is involved.

FIVE STEPS TO CREATING AND USING SCORING GUIDES

The rest of this chapter lays out five steps for designing and using scoring guides. The first step is creating a scoring guide; the other four steps deal with using it effectively. The five steps are:

Step 1. Develop a scoring guide.
Step 2. Collect or create examples of excellence.
Step 3. Have students examine and rate examples of both excellent quality and poor quality so that students learn to recognize the difference.
Step 4. Have students complete the assignment, critique their work, and revise.
Step 5. Revise the assignment and scoring guide.

Step 1. Develop a Scoring Guide

Scoring guide criteria specify what students are expected to do. If you have designed your units with the big ideas and key skills in mind, you have already done much of the analysis you need for developing a scoring guide. Once you have identified the behavior students need to demonstrate, you need to identify what performance or product you would accept as evidence that students have learned (Wiggins, 1991, 1993, 1994, 1995, 1996).

Scoring guides need to address two questions: *What do students need to learn?* and *How do students demonstrate that they have learned the big ideas and key skills required by the assignment?* Table 6.1 gives an example of a template that can be used to answer both questions.

Table 6.1. A Scoring Guide Template

Big Ideas/ Key Skills	Ways to Demonstrate Big Ideas/Key Skills	Needs Work	Meets Criteria in Part	Meets Criteria	Exceeds Criteria

To get ideas for developing a scoring guide, ask colleagues to show you examples of scoring guides they use or find templates online by searching "scoring guides" and a content area. You will find far more than you can use, and that's part of the process. Find an example you can use as an initial template and begin filling in what you know. At a minimum you need:

1. A list of big ideas or skills you will evaluate (see column 1 in Table 6.1),
2. A list of specific criteria (see column 2 in Table 6.1) that demonstrate competence and
3. A set of evaluation categories into which a product or performance fits, for example, high quality, acceptable quality, and unacceptable quality.

The process of making the guide will make you more explicit about criteria and about the big ideas and key skills you are trying to teach. As you and your students use the scoring guides, you will become aware of any changes needed.

Create categories that you and your students can easily distinguish. In some cases, a checklist may be sufficient. The product or performance either demonstrates the categories on the list or doesn't. Include only key criteria. Trying to make scoring guides overly complete can quickly become counterproductive.

There are many ways you could use the Table 6.1 template. Table 6.2, Scoring Guide: Writing a Story, is an example. The scoring guides that you develop may be much more complex than Table 6.2. Also note that criteria such as "grammatically correct" could be more specific if needed. Scoring guides can always be more specific, but it's important to settle on an appropriate level of detail.

Table 6.2. Scoring Guide: Writing a Story

Big Ideas/ Key Skills	Ways to Demonstrate Big Ideas/Key Skills	Needs Work	Meets Criteria in Part	Meets Criteria	Exceeds Criteria
Story	The story has a beginning, middle, and end.				
Imagery	Uses colorful imagery and concrete detail.				
Mechanics	Uses complete sentences.				
Punctuation	Sentences correctly punctuated.				
Spelling	Words spelled correctly.				
Grammar	Grammatically correct.				

Textbox 6.1 provides additional guidelines for making a scoring guide.

TEXTBOX 6.1. GUIDELINES FOR MAKING A SCORING GUIDE

- Keep scoring guides simple enough to grade easily but complete enough to let students know what they need to do to improve. Scoring guides that are overly detailed or complex are likely to meet with resistance from students.
- Keep scoring guides specific enough for students and parents to understand.
- Have students practice using the scoring guides. Scoring guides will be ignored by students if they do not practice using them.

You don't need to use scoring guides for everything. You may prefer to save them for major projects and performances, especially summative projects. On the other hand, if your classes do regular quizzes, labs, presentations, or short papers, you may be able to use the same scoring guides over and over. If possible, save time by putting the scoring guide right on the quiz or assignment.

Step 2. Collect or Create Examples of Excellence

If you want students to produce quality work, they need to see examples of quality work. You'll need to collect an "archive of excellence"—a library, built up over several years, of excellent work done by students and used with permission from students and their parents (Berger, 2003). For example, some schools have students make books that are put in the library for other students to see and read. (In some cases, students can pick up their work after it has been in the library for a year.) Once you start collecting quality student work (get permission from students and their parents), students can use scoring guides to get experience scoring the best work from past years.

Step 3. Have Students Rate Examples and Non-Examples of Quality Work

If you want students to produce high-quality products and performances, they need extensive exposure to excellent models—including a chance to examine, discuss, and critique those models. To succeed with as many students as possible, have students work with examples that meet criteria and examples that don't meet criteria. All students, including those who always do well, will learn to analyze and improve their work.

By giving out the scoring guides with the assignments, you let students know what they are aiming for at the beginning of their work. By having students use the scoring guides to evaluate both their own work and examples of work from past years, they can learn what they need to revise and improve.

Learning Through Analyzing

Students need practice in analyzing the criteria for the assignment. An example of how to do this is the following:

1. Students read many examples: excellent, good, and poor.
2. The teacher has a conversation with students about what makes a paper good or not so good. Don't tell students what's wrong. Ask them what's

good and what's wrong: What's good about this paper? What's not good? What could be better? What didn't the paper talk about?
3. Students use scoring guides to score the examples they have read so that they will better understand what makes a paper good or poor.
4. Students write and critique their own papers, then revise.

You'll know how many times you need to have students examine and score examples of different quality by the quality of their assignments. Once students have scored sample papers (or one another's papers), they will be more likely to use the scoring guides in preparing their work—leading, we hope, to better quality work.

Step 4. Have Students Complete the Assignment, Critique Their Work, and Revise

Students are more likely to understand scoring guide criteria and to improve their future work if they revise their present work. In addition to improving quality, student revision can make your job easier: The better the final product, the easier it will be to grade.

Option: Peer Review

The purpose of peer review is to learn how the scoring guide works through using it. It's often easier to critique someone else's paper than your own. Asking students to evaluate without the chance to improve is asking them to do something with zero payoff. Use peer review only after students have had practice in scoring examples and their own work. You want to avoid having students become confused because of inaccurate reviews.

Peer review can be tricky. Consider the following:

1. Have students do peer reviews, but never have peers grade one another. With just this one step, you avoid all sorts of potential problems.
2. Before you do peer reviews, have a conversation with students about guidelines for doing peer reviews and emphasize the importance of not criticizing or making fun of other students' work.

Revision

Allowing students to revise papers and projects can have a big payoff in stretching students to go beyond their present level of knowledge and skill. This happens all the time in sports, so we know that students can learn to value the opportunity to improve.

Of course, letting students revise everything is not always practical. You need to be selective. Experiment and see where the chance to revise results in improved learning. Chapter 9, *Help Students Learn Through Practice and Revision,* goes into the issue of revision more fully.

Step 5. Revise the Assignment and Scoring Guide

As you gain more experience from year to year, you will notice places where you want to rewrite the scoring guides. It takes about three revisions to get the criteria right, so don't be disappointed if your scoring guide doesn't work as well as you hoped. You don't have to do everything the first time you use the scoring guide.

Revise the scoring guide to reflect what you've learned about making your criteria more explicit and more helpful. As you work with learners, your understanding changes and you learn better what it is you are trying to help students learn. Over several years, your scoring guides will become more precise and more concrete.

A SCRAP OF CONVERSATION

When I first learned about scoring guides, I realized that I had graded thousands of papers but very few of the papers I returned left students knowing what they could have done better. Then when I started creating scoring guides, I found that being explicit about scoring criteria was very tough. Now you can go online and find scoring guides for every level and subject. Back then you had to struggle on your own—except for schools who really got it; they would have a book of scoring guides for their teachers to learn from. With every round of using a scoring guide, you learn more about what wasn't on the scoring guide that needed to be there. The scoring guides make you a better observer; they help you become more explicit about what you're trying to do and how it is working.

CONCLUSION

Doing quality work is a circular process that involves practice in identifying, critiquing, and revising work. It's easy to underestimate the need to be explicit when helping students understand quality work. We can't know what students can do until they've learned to recognize quality and then revise their own work until it meets the standard of quality.

Setting up assignments and writing scoring guides may be time consuming, but each time you use the assignment, you will learn how to improve the assignment and the scoring guide. The extra work you put in will pay off because as the model examples of student work, the assignments, and the scoring guides all improve, your job will be easier and current student work will improve over previous years.

Save the best examples of each assignment so that you have examples to show students next time you give the assignment. If you save the best examples of work from your classes and use those as models, the quality of work will go up. Be sure to get students' written permission to use their assignments in writing.

While scoring guides are a way to give grades, their big contribution is in teaching students what to pay attention to, thus the importance of having students rate examples of varying quality. Through the rating process—including small-group and class conversation—students are learning how to learn.

Q & A

Q. *If students see all these great models, won't they copy them?*
A. They won't copy them—or if they do, it will be obvious and you can have them revise their work. They will tend to imitate the models—and that's a good thing. Your better students are the ones who are already familiar with models because they're the ones who read on their own, have had stories read to them, have been to museums, and so on. The poorer students won't have the advantage of having models to imitate because they don't come to school already having experienced them. That hardly seems fair. On the other hand, if you provide excellent models, even the good students will profit from discussing and critiquing them.

Q. *Isn't it difficult and subjective to evaluate higher-order objectives?*
A. It's not that much more difficult to write and test for higher-order objectives if you focus on the products and performances you would like to see from students. If you also teach students to use the scoring guides and you require them to revise, they learn what they need to do and they can learn to do better work.

Q. *I don't know if I want to use scoring guides for everything I do.*
A. Use scoring guides for those major assignments and tests and wherever students need to revise to improve their skills of reading, writing, thinking, and presenting. Not everything needs to be—or is worth—revising. You decide.

ADDITIONAL RESOURCES

Berger, R. (2003). *An ethic of excellence*. Portsmouth, NH: Heinemann.

An outstanding reference for helping students do quality work by using examples and non-examples. Berger creates what he calls "an archive of excellence." Berger spends an entire chapter on the archives of student work he uses to teach students, parents, teachers, administrators, and members of the community what students can do when they care about their work.

Newmann, F., & Wehlage, G. (1993). Five standards of authentic instruction. *Educational Leadership, 50*, 8–12. http://www.learner.org/workshops/socialstudies/pdf/session6/6.AuthenticInstruction.pdf

A short and very helpful framework for planning that includes five standards: (1) higher-order thinking, (2) depth of knowledge, (3) connectedness to the world, (4) substantive conversation, and (5) social support for achievement.

Chapter Seven

Motivation Follows Action

"To motivate learners, get them to act."

—Robert J. Martin

If you want to motivate students, an excellent plan is contained in this book's subtitle, *Connect with Students and Involve Them in Learning.* We need to involve students in learning because they learn more and because they are more motivated to learn. Motivation and learning are intertwined; the relationship is one of circularity. When we involve students in learning, they feel more motivated and connected. When students feel more motivated and connected, they are more willing to become involved.

I remember Tom, an eighth-grader who was not motivated to work in school. Yet he was committed to getting up at five o'clock in the morning to participate in a community basketball league. He didn't think twice about getting up to do what he wanted—play basketball. The emotion and the involvement were there, so the difficulties and frustrations of learning basketball were no problem for him. School was another matter; there, he was overwhelmed by a degree of difficulty and frustration that was no more daunting than learning to play basketball. Tom felt connected to basketball, but not to school.

IF YOU WANT TO FEEL MOTIVATED, ACT

If you want your students to feel motivated, have them act. The typical understanding of motivation is that action follows motivation. It is true that we sometimes act because we feel motivated, but we don't have to feel motivated to act. This is why it is so important to get students (and ourselves) to act, and to act in a way that actions become habits that, like getting up in the morning, we do without thinking. This chapter and the six chapters that follow are concerned with ways to motivate students by getting them to act.

To Get Students Motivated, Get Them to Act

We've all spent time creating what we thought were exciting, interesting lessons, only to have students yawn or roll their eyes. Instead, focus on what you can have students do. This chapter focuses on quick and easy ways to induce action. Each of the remaining chapters goes into detail regarding specific topics: procedures to automate actions, practice and revision, team learning and practice, conversation, and presentations that involve students. When you first get students involved, they may complain that you're making them do something, but if you stick to your plan, and you get them involved in acting on a regular basis, they'll complain if you stop and don't involve them.

Physical Warm-Ups to Get Students Involved

When we move, our thinking and our perception change. Sometimes just moving for a few minutes is enough of a break to get students (or ourselves) working again, whether they're first-graders or seniors in high school. If you're using team activities (see Chapters 10 and 11) or getting students into small groups for short conversation activities (see Chapter 12), students are already moving.

Warm-up activities can be a way of easing into difficult work or a way of taking a break in the middle of difficult work. The simplest warm-up activities involve having students stand up and stretch. Do an isometric exercise (joining your hands together and pulling in opposite directions), or shake out feet, hands, and fingers. You do it and the students imitate. We know it works because we've done it as students.

You can find additional warm-up activities online by searching "warm-up activities" in your browser. Keep in mind that you are using warm-up activities to increase productivity by getting students mentally ready to pay attention.

With older students, be prepared for them to resist—moving can feel silly or embarrassing or stupid. You may be taking some students out of their comfort zones—which may take you out of your comfort zone, so be prepared to look and feel silly. Once, at a rural school, I and my night extension class of in-service teachers were forbidden from using a new library room after the superintendent observed us hopping around the library on invisible pogo sticks as a warmup to a serious conversation on problems of teaching. He never said anything directly, but apparently, we were way too active.

Mental Warm-Ups to Get an Activity Started

Select activities from the checklist below to use as warm-ups in your classroom. Try a variety of strategies to see what works best to get your students ready for learning:

- Ask students to share their pictures regarding a topic.
- Share an example and then ask for an example.
- Have students draw a diagram or make an outline.
- Have students write in a journal.
- Have students do several minutes of automatic writing about the topic without stopping.
- Individually or in teams, brainstorm a list of ideas related to the task.
- Each student makes their own list on a topic, then teams consolidate lists into a master list.

Take a Break or Change Activities

A change of activity is experienced as a break, and a break is a reward. When students are giving their full attention to a task or a speaker, ten to twenty minutes (depending on student age) is considered a maximum attention span. Short breaks may be helpful when students are becoming frustrated or inattentive.

Use Social Rewards Rather Than Material Rewards

Material rewards always imply evaluation, and neither children nor adults like to take risks if they are going to be evaluated or if they are going for a big reward. (Notice that in the Winter Olympics, the figure skaters who take risks are usually those who are already out of the running for a gold medal.) Evaluations, even if in the form of praise, can discourage students from participating (Martin, 1980). Another problem with evaluating student input is that if you do not praise every answer, lack of praise becomes a condemnation: *"Teacher did not say my answer was good. I don't understand what was wrong with it."*

Social rewards—interactions that create well-being—work better than material rewards, are easy to implement, and are more fun. Praise participation rather than correctness: "Thanks for volunteering" is participation centered; "Good answer" is correctness centered, even if you do not mean it to be. If you give praise, say what was done well: "Your poem shows imagination" rather than a general "Good job."

DESIGN TASKS THAT GET STUDENTS TO ACT

The strategies that follow are a chance to review what you're already doing and reflect on where you may want to make a change.

Break Choices and Tasks Into Smaller Steps When Necessary

If you want to motivate students—or yourself—to do something, you need to break it down into small steps that do not evoke fear and resistance—and then practice those behaviors until they become automated. What constitutes a small step is determined by the grade and the ability of the students. Pick a step that is so small that you can get all the students to do it.

Scheduling is part of breaking choices and tasks into smaller steps. Break difficult tasks down into components that are easy to do, then schedule them in short blocks with the most difficult chunk first (if the chunks don't have to be sequential). We tend to like activities we do well and to do well at activities we like. Since liking encourages effort that leads to doing well and doing well encourages liking, use small steps and limited commitments to increase both success and liking.

Design Choices

If you know some students will have problems making choices or doing tasks, you can put everyone through a procedure as a class that helps them narrow down their choices (the next chapter is all about procedures). This will help everyone, not just the students having problems. Where assignments are problematic for part of the class, create a series of questions, structured choices, or smaller tasks that help students narrow down how to proceed. When you step students through a procedure many times, they learn to handle larger steps on their own.

Some students won't have a sufficiently large album of mental pictures (or the fund of knowledge) they need to choose a topic. Some students may have a large album of mental pictures but have difficulty making a choice. Confronted with a large restaurant menu, I used to have problems making a choice, even as an adult. I learned to force myself to make a choice in a given amount of time. In working with students who have trouble making a choice, ask them questions about their interests. Then give them a list of three possible topics based on their interests and ask them to choose one. These are just examples—you can create appropriate ways to break tasks into smaller steps when you see students getting stuck.

Design Tasks

The most important thing in teaching is structuring the learning process effectively. If you continually observe what students can do, you can design tasks that require them to go a level that is just beyond their current level. You can learn what's needed only through observing, reflecting, and experimenting—and continually stepping outside your comfort zone.

Avoid Making Lessons Too Easy—or Too Difficult

Engage learners below the threshold where actions are so hard that they give up and above the threshold where actions are so easy that they become boring because there's no challenge (Vygotsky, 1978). As already mentioned, we tend to like what we do well and to do well what we like. Help students be successful and they'll be more likely to keep working. Our job is to consider the strengths of the individual or group and then to choose a task or activity that is most likely to produce a result that is satisfying and successful.

Success by itself is not sufficient to create motivation; the task cannot be too easy or students will quit. The goal is to create assignments that can be done by all learners at each learner's present level of ability and that gets students to go just beyond their current level. Think of this as a direction to go in rather than a predetermined answer. Creating scoring guides (see the previous chapter) can give you experience in going in this direction.

Give Students Enough Time to Complete Tasks

Pressuring students to complete an activity in five minutes that needs ten minutes is self-defeating. On the other hand, providing fifteen minutes for a task that only needs ten for thoughtful completion is deenergizing and easily leads to behavior problems. Experiment and then make notes on your lesson plans about what worked and what didn't.

Get a Ten-Minute Commitment

Ten-minute commitments are one way to get students to face difficult tasks. Learners who are already discouraged are not up to big commitments. What constitutes a "big commitment" is determined solely by what students feel they can handle. For some students, writing a page is a big commitment; for others, writing a paragraph is a big commitment. When students are not succeeding at the task you are giving them because they are overwhelmed, ask for a limited commitment designed so they can meet it successfully.

If a ten-minute commitment is too big, try a five-minute or even a one-minute commitment. You're trying to get a student who has given up and refuses to work to do something. It doesn't matter how small that something is; once it is done, you can go for another something, and another, and so on. This may not be completely rational, but it sometimes works even on students who are adamant about not trying.

Short commitments can work well with a whole class, especially if you give them a short time to do a task and then move on to the next task. You can judge how long "ten minutes" is by watching how well students are succeeding in completing a task. If they need more time, you can give them a one-minute warning and then give them an extra minute. If they aren't going to need ten minutes, you can give them a one-minute warning at eight minutes, for a total of nine minutes.

Table 7.1 provides several examples of short commitments. Review the sample items to see if there are changes you can make in your expectations to encourage students to stick with challenging tasks.

Table 7.1. Short Tasks to Decrease Discouragement

Instead of This:	Do This First:
Read a chapter of dense prose.	Read one page.
Do a book report.	Write about what you liked in the book.
Do a page of math problems.	Do three problems in the next ten minutes.
Organize a notebook.	Go through notebook; throw away unneeded papers.
Write on a topic for twenty minutes once a week.	Write in a notebook every day for five minutes.

Premack: Eat Dessert Last

A good way to get students to act when they don't feel like it is by using Premacking (named for David Premack, the psychologist who described the technique), otherwise known as Grandma's Rule. Grandma's Rule is that you eat dessert last. The goal is to get students in the habit of finishing difficult tasks before doing tasks that are easier and/or more fun. This is an easy technique to use—and it works! As children, we (hopefully) learn to eat the main course before we eat dessert. We would think it strange to reverse this order. Yet both teachers and students do just this when they promise themselves: *"I'll just sit down and watch this TV program and then do my homework."*

Do Less-Disliked Tasks Last

Doing more pleasant tasks first kills off motivation to finish less pleasant tasks. Premacking makes use of this idea by doing tasks in order from least liked to most liked. Premacking can be used with individual students or an entire class. The technique is very simple: Do unpleasant or disliked tasks first. Premacking creates motivation by structuring tasks from least liked to most liked. Each task becomes a reward for the task preceding it. Never reward behavior before it is completed, as when we promise ourselves that we'll do a difficult task after we do something fun.

To get experience with the technique, Premack yourself to tackle tasks you tend to avoid, whatever they might be—paying bills, balancing your checkbook, exercising, cleaning off your desk. Do the task you're avoiding before you do a more pleasant task. Using Premacking, I trained myself to do our income taxes early. Learn to Premack yourself and you'll figure out how to Premack your students. Also, teaching yourself to Premack makes you aware of how teachers have the same problems as students.

Teach Students—and Parents—to Premack Homework

Premacking homework is an excellent strategy for all students, but especially those who are not getting their homework done. The following three-step process is a great strategy to teach students and their parents. The technique requires ordering a list from most liked to least liked and then doing the tasks in the reverse order, starting with the least liked. (In some cases, the student doesn't like any of the choices, so "most liked" is more accurately described as "least disliked." For example, who wants to do homework of any sort?) Here is the list of steps:

Step 1. Student Makes a List of Tasks That Need to Be Done

- Play videogames (Remember this is the student's list!)
- Math homework
- English homework
- Social studies homework

Step 2. Student Prioritizes the List From Most Liked to Least Liked

If student hates some or all of them, one will still be least hated.

Likes best: Play videogames
Like second best: English homework
Like third best: Social studies homework
Like least: Math homework

Step 3. Student Does the List in Reverse Order

Do first: Math homework
Do second: Social studies homework

Do third: English homework
Do fourth: Videogames

In the above list, doing social studies homework isn't much of a reward for doing math homework, but that's not the point. When we do what we most want to avoid first, we'll still tend to go ahead and do the other things on our list. If necessary, it's okay to take short breaks in between tasks—though a change of activity is also a way to take a break.

Keep in mind that a list from best liked to least liked is going to be different for each student. Also, unless you take students through the steps and then get them started on the least-liked homework, they're probably not going to follow through—unless you've gone through the procedure at a parent-teacher conference and gotten the parents' cooperation. Establishing a habit is not easy, and there are no guarantees that a particular approach will work with a given student. On the other hand, at least in elementary school, it's traditional to put the most difficult subject in the morning before lunch. Now you know the reason.

HELP STUDENTS REALIZE IT'S OKAY IF YOU DON'T FEEL LIKE IT

Feeling like doing something is not a necessary condition for action. We may not feel like going to work, but we get up anyway, without thinking about it, because we have the habit of going to work. Helping students to acquire this same habit is what we're after here. We can help students learn that the best way to deal with a lack of motivation is to choose to act anyway. How? Let students know it's okay to feel like not doing a task—but they can still do it.

You can help students dispute the mistaken belief that they can't act unless they feel like it. For example, you can ask, "Does not wanting to finish your paper prevent you from finishing?" The rational answer is, "No." The question needs to be said in a neutral way so that it doesn't sound like blaming, because blaming kills motivation and cooperation.

Being explicit about the fact that feelings do not have to control actions can help both teachers and students finish their work when they don't feel like it. For example, even students who refuse to do a lick of work in school because they do not like school may:

- go to basketball practice when they are on the team,
- show up for work to keep an afterschool job,
- speak respectfully to a police officer, boss, or teacher to stay out of trouble.

Students can sometimes see things from a more objective point of view when they imagine other students having the same problem and are asked to give advice to that student. For example, you can say, "What would you say if a friend told you he wanted a good grade but was having problems finishing a project?"

Students need to realize that adults may also find their work difficult. Several years ago, two authors of children's books, Ann Hadley and Lee Irwin, spoke to students about the books they had written. They talked with great enthusiasm about writing. They also talked about the manuscripts of books they had written that were never published and about how difficult it was to complete a book. They admitted to one young reader, "It doesn't get easier. Each one is just as difficult as the first."

Help Students Move Beyond Fear

We all have students who don't like to do new things—including good students who don't like to take risks. It's okay to ask students to do things that feel scary but are not dangerous. Doing something is always more terrifying than doing nothing, but in the end, it's more satisfying. When students fear failure, they resist acting. If doing something, no matter how easy, evokes fear, we resist. If the fear is intense, we shut down and refuse to budge. The bigger the change, the more fear that is evoked and the more we resist. Hence the reason for small changes that encourage teachers and students to ignore fear and act anyway.

A SCRAP OF CONVERSATION

Sometimes I would be given a student who had given up on math. There was nothing magic I could say that would convince him or her otherwise. Instead, I might have them count by twos: two, four, six, eight, up to a hundred. For an older student, we might go on counting by threes or fours, depending on how far they had gotten with their multiplication tables. I would say with conviction, "This shows that you are smarter than you think you are." They couldn't deny the truth: They had just done something they didn't think they could do. Find something a student can do and be successful and you may have a chance, no matter how far behind the student is. When students have given up, the first step is to convince them that they are smarter and more capable than they think.

After having been on stage in many different roles, I've become comfortable with doing just about anything, no matter how silly it looks. However, I didn't start out this way. I resisted change. I started out very shy and uncomfortable and afraid of looking stupid. To get students to step out of their comfort zone, you have to step outside yours. The good stuff is just beyond your comfort zone.

CONCLUSION

We do not need to feel motivated to act; we need to act to feel motivated. To motivate students, identify small actions that lead to success, then have students practice those actions until they become habits.

Have a student perform a small action that leads to success and—if the student can do this consistently—you have a recipe for creating motivation. Clear enough, but like all good ideas, easier said than done. Pick easy tasks that do not evoke fear and resistance. Be willing to keep simplifying tasks even beyond what you think is reasonable until you find something the student agrees to do—and does.

Let students know that it is okay for them not to like working on a project, as long as they keep working. This removes some of the pressure of "you not only have to do this, but you also have to like it, too." Use Premacking to help teach the habit of not avoiding things by first doing things students most want to avoid. In other words, have students eat dessert last.

Q & A

Q. *If I build in short breaks, won't my students just end up getting off-task? Won't that lead to a waste of teaching time?*

A. Yes, that can happen. Decide, based on your own observation, how long students can go before they start losing attention. One way to take a break without taking a break is to switch to another activity that keeps students on-task while serving as a break from a more difficult activity. There's nothing to say that the short break can't focus on the material being learned. For example, students can take a break from reading or listening to lecture to summarize what they've learned to a partner. This provides a break and solidifies learning. Chapter 13 presents a variety of ways of involving students when you are presenting information. The short activities give students a break from listening to new information while simultaneously involving them more deeply in the content.

Q. *Some students refuse to do anything. What do I do with a student who won't act?*
A. There are no easy answers. Keep offering alternatives without getting into a power struggle. If you're in a power struggle, a student may avoid doing anything just to defeat you. Stay cheerful, inviting, and encouraging. Beyond this, the best thing to do is to keep trying to find out: What is this student willing to do? What interests this student? What does she do outside the class? What do I know about this student? Who are his friends? Am I developing a positive relationship with this student?

ADDITIONAL RESOURCES

Organizations and Conferences in Your Grade or Subject Area

The best possible way to explore ways to get your students involved is to go to a regional or national conference in your area. Going to conferences where teachers present exciting projects and activities they are doing with their students is a way to get ideas, inspiration, and know-how. Type the name of the professional organization in your area and the word "conference" into your browser and see what is available.

Glasser Institute for Choice Theory. National Conference for Choice Theory. https://wglasser.com/events/national-conference-for-choice-theory/

Many of the hands-on-approaches, procedures, and activities in this book came from attending the annual national Glasser Institute conferences, participating in a wide variety of activities during presentations and workshops, and then coming back and trying these activities with teacher education students and in-service teachers and public school students.

National Science Teaching Association. Conferences. https://www.nsta.org/conferences/national.aspx/

The National Science Teaching Association conferences (mentioned in Chapter 1) are an example of an opportunity to learn from others in an area and grade level. Even if you're the only person in your school who is working to involve your students more actively, the experience of being in the same venue with hundreds or even thousands of teachers in your area will be amazing and encouraging.

Chapter Eight

Increase Learning by Teaching Procedures

"Do the same steps every time, all the time."

—Anonymous

Effective learning is built on lower-level procedures that help learners focus on more complex tasks. Like all skills, procedures are best taught through modeling, practice, and monitoring. When we learn to brush our teeth, spell a word, drive a car, use a fork, or write a paper, we are learning to automate a procedure or a set of procedures. As those procedures become automated and modified, they become the basis of powerful skills. Even the smallest procedure is important in allowing us to focus on bigger things.

Learning to use a fork once took a big effort and we didn't do it very well. After doing it for some time, we got better at it and we now do it automatically—even perfectly—as do our students. The power of taking a small step comes from repeating it. Once you repeat the same small step every day (or as often as the class meets), you've created a procedure. Once you've created a procedure, if you do it regularly, it becomes automated and you can build on it do to more complex tasks. Once a step has become easier, you can make the step bigger. For example, once students can spell, they can focus on writing words, phrases, and sentences instead of individual letters.

Once the work of creating a habit has been accomplished, the results can be quite striking. In one high school class, the students had a work period where they were expected to write. The students were noisy, distracted, and not doing much writing. In another high school in the same city, the students came into class, sat down, took out their journals, and wrote. (*Everyone* wrote—I walked around and saw lots of very full pages.) Clearly, the second teacher had spent a lot of time and effort connecting with students and establishing the procedure that students were following.

WHY TEACH PROCEDURES

Far from killing creativity or discouraging higher-order learning, teaching procedures allows you to do more creative, complex lessons. Structure is a friend of creativity and higher-order thinking. This is just as valid for high school students and adults as it is for elementary and middle school students.

Procedures Free Teachers and Students

A procedure is a schema—a set of behaviors that allows us to perform complex tasks that we do automatically and hardly ever think about (such as walk, run, type, write, read, and so on). When we drive, the small adjustments we make to the steering wheel keep us on the road. We make these adjustments without thinking; we just pay attention to the road and where we're going and the adjustments seem to happen. This is true for all skills and this is the direction in which we can take students because automated procedures that become skills allow students to go a bit beyond where they are.

We live immersed in a sea of procedures that allow us to go about our business. Since we typically learn these procedures through immersion and modeling, we have little awareness of them. Begin to become explicitly aware of them and you'll have a much easier time seeing where individual students, and your class as a whole, need procedures to participate and learn more effectively.

When procedures become automated, they allow students to learn more efficiently. For example, students have trouble thinking about sentences and paragraphs until recognition of words and phrases becomes automatic. Students can't efficiently write what they think until spelling becomes automatic. Students can't carry out long division efficiently until adding, subtracting, and multiplying become automatic. Procedures allow students to think and act in more complex ways.

Teaching procedures helps both you and your students use class time more productively. Procedures can remove unnecessary decision making—students don't have to think about what to do next. Turning instructions into procedures makes instructions more effective—students know the drill and can go right to whatever they need to do. Teaching procedures for transitions can reduce transition time—students know what to do and they do it.

Teach Procedures So You Can Increase Involvement

You already teach some procedures and your students learn them; the purpose here is to become more explicit so that you are more able to create and use procedures to involve students in new ways. For example, the next two chapters focus on the benefits and the nuts and bolts of team learning.

Procedures that you use over and over make it possible to do more complicated activities without confusion. For example, team learning is an effective way to increase the amount of time students spend practicing key skills and big ideas. However, without knowing and teaching procedures that make team learning work, teachers have little success in using team learning and tend to abandon it after the first few times. Yet I have observed well-educated teacher interns do an exemplary job using team learning procedures.

SECRETS OF USING PROCEDURES

Procedures require an investment of time. You have to figure out the steps of the procedure (or learn an existing procedure), create clear instructions, and then walk students through the procedure numerous times until your instructions and student actions become automated.

Become Comfortable With Being Uncomfortable

Like doing any new procedure (such as using a new online banking procedure or a grading system), we never get it right the first time. We have to do it repeatedly until it becomes familiar—and that's uncomfortable. The secret to getting better at using new procedures is becoming comfortable with being uncomfortable. If you want to never make mistakes and look perfect, you won't do anything new. The first step is realizing that being uncomfortable and making mistakes is part of the process. That's the wonderful thing about learning new procedures at conferences and workshops: It's a low-risk situation where you learn by doing and no one notices your struggles or mistakes. But then after you do it, you have experienced that procedure, and with a bit of effort, you can teach your students to do it.

Since human beings don't do things right the first time, whether they're teachers or students, how can we do a better job at helping students to follow directions and procedures? The following guidelines can be helpful.

Small Changes Take Effect Only If Students Practice Them Repeatedly

I heard William Glasser say, "The problem with good ideas is that you have to do them." If you help students practice even very small changes in how they do their work, you will see results. And if you don't, you can try other small changes until you find something that works. It may take several weeks of practice before students can do even a simple procedure correctly and efficiently. Don't give up. Even older students may not do what you ask until they've practiced repeatedly.

Step Students Through the Procedure You Want Them to Learn

I used to explain to students that we were going to get into groups of two and that they needed to pair up with a student they didn't usually work with. I would then ask them to go ahead and find a partner—and no one would move. And these were college students preparing to be teachers! Now I say, "Okay, everyone, stand up!"—and I wait until everyone stands up, which takes quite a while the first time. At the beginning, it's all one step at a time and you don't move on to the next step until everyone has done that step.

Prepare Thoroughly and You Feel More Relaxed and in Control

We usually think of preparing as something we do because the job requires it. Here's an additional way to think about preparing: Preparing is something you do for yourself. It's a gift you give yourself. If you notice how much better you feel when you are prepared, you will find it easier to prepare. This was brought home to me when I started doing community theatre. Intense fear motivated me to prepare very, very thoroughly.

Fear was a big motivator because standing in front of four hundred ticket holders is a lot scarier than standing in front of a class. But then, I found that the better prepared I was, the less nervous and more secure I was. I found that I liked performing. As a result of this very intense experience, I noticed the same phenomenon with my classes: I always felt better when I was better prepared. I'm sure I knew this before, but I didn't notice it.

Preparing leads to experiencing the joy of being well prepared. Of course, sometimes we can be well prepared and things don't go at all well. That is to be expected. It goes with the territory. And knowing that it is to be expected can help us to still keep preparing as well as we can.

HOW TO TEACH PROCEDURES

Teaching procedures is always a circular interaction between teacher and students. You see how it goes and then you adjust accordingly. The six tasks that follow provide guidance.

Task 1. Teach the Same Steps Every Time, All the Time

Some years ago, I needed advice on raising a twenty-seven-foot mast on a small catamaran—a dangerous undertaking. I bought a piece of equipment and then contacted its maker by phone to get his advice for using the equipment safely. He changed how I look at procedures of all kinds when he said: *"Do the same steps every time, all the time."* With this small sentence, the man reframed how I look at any repeated task, from playing the piano to setting up a small sailboat mast to stepping students through a procedure. The idea of procedures was not new, but I had always resisted learning procedures as boring and uncreative. The experience of dealing with a dangerous situation enabled me to reframe.

Walk Students through Procedures One Step at a Time

When you're teaching a procedure, guide students one step at a time. This uses the minimum amount of time to do an activity. It also allows you to better monitor the activity and cuts down on confusion. Sometimes what we think is too simple and obvious is appropriate not only for younger students but for older students and even adults as well. This was exemplified by the choir director who asked his college choir members to take out their pencils every time before telling them what to mark in their music. Figuring out what the steps are in a procedure takes not only thought but observation of what isn't working—in this case, choir members not marking music because they don't have their pencils out or maybe don't even have pencils.

Take a Pencil, Leave a Shoe

A high school teacher kept a box of pencils for students to borrow for occasions when they would say, "I don't have a pencil." He went through dozens of pencils before coming up with a simple procedure: I loan you a pencil; you leave a personal article to be retrieved when you return the pencil—an ID, a phone, a shoe. Funny and effective. Takeaway: Procedures are developed over time through experience.

Teach Procedures through Modeling and Practice

Learning and following a set of instructions is a skill, and, like all skills, is best learned through modeling, practice, and feedback over days or weeks. Rehearse procedures when they aren't working; if they still don't work, redesign them.

Human beings are not good at following even simple instructions until they have rehearsed them. This applies to adults just as much as it does to students (Wong & Wong, 2018). When students aren't following instructions, then you need to do what bands, choirs, directors, and football coaches do: Rehearse until everyone knows the drill.

Expect Twenty or More Repetitions to Make a Procedure a Habit

When you try a new procedure with your students, make sure directions are clear and don't expect it to work perfectly the first time or even the tenth time—it may or may not take more practice. Human beings are not good at following directions unless they practice. This applies to adults and children, teachers and students. Yet learning procedures is mostly taken for granted; it seems to be a topic reserved for kindergarten teachers and neurosurgeons. What applies to kindergarten teachers and neurosurgeons applies to all grades and contents: Procedures need to be clear and have to be practiced until learned.

Task 2. Prepare Instructions Ahead of Time—and Rehearse Them

Knowing what you want students to do is not the same as knowing what instructions you are going to give. If students are having trouble following your instructions, you need to write out the instructions (3×5 cards often work well). Eventually, you won't need them—you'll have them memorized.

Do most teachers write out instructions? Probably not. However, in many cases, their students become confused—and the teacher doesn't even notice. If you take the trouble to figure out the simplest and most direct instructions, you are more likely to notice when students are confused. In the process, you will master the art of creating and giving clear instructions. It may take a little more time, but it is an investment in becoming a master teacher.

Task 3. Keep Instructions Simple and Do Not Overexplain

Break instructions into simple steps and then lead students through those instructions one step at a time. As you automate your instruction-giving behavior, you will be better able to increase your "withitness"—the ability to monitor behavior in the classroom (Kounin, 1970). Withitness is neither a magical skill nor a matter of good intentions—it is a matter of preparing so thoroughly that your attention can be on your students.

Give Directions Once

Give instructions once and do not repeat them; repeating instructions teaches students not to listen the first time. If necessary, ask a student to repeat the instructions to the class as soon as you give them. Giving instructions only once is a good strategy to increase attending behavior by increasing accountability.

Put Complicated, Multistep Instructions in Writing

You will probably still need to step students through complicated instructions verbally, but if you put them in writing, students can refer to the written instructions as needed. Make allowances for students who are not able to follow instructions. Think of this not as a discipline problem but as a problem of insufficient rehearsal—students have not yet practiced a procedure enough to follow it. There can be many reasons students have trouble understanding and following procedures, including lack of English proficiency, lack of experience, and lack of practice. Even a big game or an upcoming three-day weekend can make it difficult for students to focus and follow instructions.

Try using "three before me," a procedure developed by Kagan and Kagan (2017): Students must ask three other students before asking the teacher. Be prepared, however, to have students ignore this procedure unless you enforce it by not answering.

Task 4. Tell Students What You Want, Not What You Don't Want

Human beings cannot practice negative actions. If they receive a negative instruction, they need to stop what they're doing and figure out what to do. For example, if you say, "Don't run," some who aren't running will hear the word run and may even start to run. A few may stop. Others will continue running. Better to say, "Walk!" Students need to be able to picture what you are asking.

Show Examples Rather Than Giving Complex Instructions

It is much easier to get students to make a paper airplane by showing them a model than to give instructions on how to make it. Keep this principle in mind and you'll focus more on showing students examples and less on explaining what you want.

Task 5. Help Students Stay Calm and in Control of Their Actions

Students can learn simple procedures that allow them to stay calm in difficult situations. For example, some students have test anxiety. Teachers can help by giving them a procedure to stay calm. The following three-step procedure is an example:

Step 1. Invite everyone in the class to imagine an activity they feel confident doing—playing basketball, fishing, hunting, playing a game, cooking—it doesn't matter what it is. You don't need to know what it is.

Step 2. Ask the students to imagine doing that activity. Ask them to pay attention to how they feel—for example, relaxed and confident—when they're doing this activity.

Step 3. Lastly, ask students to keep imagining the same activity as they take the test.

Task 6. Teach Students Procedures That Empower Them

Teaching students to think of mistakes as learning opportunities is an effective strategy to empower students who tend to give up. Carol Dweck used this strategy to get students to embrace challenges and work on problems that were slightly beyond where they were at the time. Dweck (2007) found that students tend to think they can't do something because they don't have the ability. Teaching students to think of a challenge as something that they are not yet able to do helped them work hard to solve the problems slightly beyond them.

TEACH PROCEDURES THAT HELP STUDENTS ORGANIZE

Helping students organize helps you. Establish procedures that teach students to organize their work. For example: Have students regularly clean out their desks, lockers, and notebooks, encouraging them to throw away anything they do not need. Even in middle school students need to be given explicit steps for doing this.

Sample procedure: Have students separate papers into three piles: Papers to take home to parents, papers to throw away, and papers to keep for study in a notebook. Then have them throw away the papers in the throwaway pile, organize the study pile for the next exam in their notebook, and put the papers for parents pile in their backpack on top of their other books.

The right way to organize is whatever allows you and your students to work effectively and to enjoy the work. When a person becomes unproductive because of poor organization, it is time to change. Sometimes even a small change can produce a large increase in productivity. The most important change, however, is seeing the organization of time, place, and materials as part of the work itself, not something added.

A SCRAP OF CONVERSATION

Sometimes even the simplest procedures need to be practiced. Teachers would let me know that a student I was counseling wasn't turning in assignments. The student had finished the assignment but lost track of it and didn't turn it in. I would supervise the student as he (these were always male students) went through a hopelessly full notebook, backpack, locker (yes, locker; some of the students were middle-schoolers) as he threw away assignments long ago returned by the teacher or old papers finished but never turned in (when it was too late to turn them in). He wasn't mean or rebellious, he just lacked procedures for organizing his stuff.

CONCLUSION

Almost everything we do from the time we get up in the morning until we go to bed at night is built on procedures. Socialized as we are, we are seldom aware of how many of the things we do are procedures. Become aware of problems that result from lack of skills, experience, and practice, and you will be better able to design procedures that help students.

If you do the work of developing clear instructions, you will develop world-class sensitivity to the language of instructions—and after a while, you will no longer need to write out instructions for most things. You will be much more aware of where confusion arises and how to avoid it. Your skill will also make it much easier to direct adult activities should you be asked to do so.

Q & A

Q. *Isn't teaching procedures going to take time?*
A. You don't necessarily need to spend extra time teaching procedures. It will take some extra time for you to figure out what procedures you need and what the steps will be, but once you do that, you're going to start saving time almost immediately.

Q. *Procedures are an important part of learning mathematics or music, but what procedures are involved in learning subjects like history, social studies, science, or language arts?*
A. In addition to procedures like where to put your name and how to format papers, every subject area has procedures such as how to research a topic and write it up, how to do a presentation, how to do a lab and write up a lab report, how to use technology, how to format a problem or paper, how to do team learning (covered in Chapters 10 and 11), how to format references in history, how to take notes, how to summarize what the previous person said, and so on.

Q. *Can teaching procedures have an impact on discipline?*
A. Procedures allow you to keep the class moving and productive—which can help prevent or reduce disciplinary problems. Procedures clarify expectations and help eliminate confusion and off-task behavior.

ADDITIONAL RESOURCES

Wong, H. K., & Wong, R. (2018). *The first days of school: How to be an effective teacher* (5th ed.). Mountain View, CA: Harry K. Wong.

Wong's focus is on specific procedures that may seem trivial, but which add up to saving time and sanity. You can also find Harry Wong videos on YouTube.

Chapter Nine

Help Students Learn Through Practice and Revision

All good teaching is coaching.

—Suzanne Martin

Practice needs to be meaningful, frequent, and focused; it needs to concentrate on what learners cannot yet do. Practice needs to be challenging without becoming discouraging—neither too difficult nor too easy. All this is a tall order, which is why as teachers we are continually learning how to design procedures that engage students in effective practice.

GUIDELINES FOR PRACTICE

We learn in proportion to the amount of time we spend practicing the things we have trouble doing (Colvin, 2010). Successful people put in large amounts of time practicing what they don't yet do well; those same people also enjoy the fruits of being good at something.

Find Out What Students Don't Understand

Deciding what to practice begins with finding out what students don't understand. To succeed with students who are having difficulties learning, get to know as much as possible about four questions:

- What are students not understanding?
- What skills do students need to improve?

- What necessary prior knowledge are students missing?
- What will help students most?

An Example of Missing Prior Knowledge: Understanding Nick

The better we understand our students, the more likely we are to be able to design lessons that lead to understanding and improved skills. The following is an example of a student who was failing in part because of a lack of understanding of the problem in the textbook that he was expected to address. Nick was a second-grader who was very frustrated and was making poor decisions—otherwise, he wouldn't have been seeing me.

Nick didn't understand what he was being asked to do. The problem he was trying to read in his math text seemed appropriate for a second-grader, but in fact, it made no sense to him. The problem called for students to understand a two-dimensional table arrayed as in Table 9.1.

Table 9.1. Nick's Bus Schedule

BUS SCHEDULE			
Day of Week	Time		
Monday	7:00 a.m.	1:00 p.m.	5:00 p.m.
Wednesday	9:00 a.m.	2:00 p.m.	5:00 p.m.
Friday	8:00 a.m.	3:00 p.m.	5:00 p.m.

Nick did not understand the table, so I showed him how the table was put together and how to read the table. He did not get it. We were not getting anywhere, so I began to think, *What does it take to understand and read this table?* It takes familiarity with buses and bus schedules. This student lived in a rural area and rode a school bus but had no other experience with buses or bus schedules and how they work, so it is understandable that he didn't understand the problem.

Minor detective work was all that was necessary to find out at least part of the problem. We then talked about living in a big city and what it would be like to get around by bus and how one would need to understand the bus schedule. With this conversation out of the way, we were then able to discuss the bus schedule and how it worked.

Connect Practice to Students' Worlds

Part of connecting with students and getting to know them (discussed in Chapter 2) is getting to know their funds of knowledge and how these connect with school learning. We need to connect practice to the world of each student, including their interests, culture, language, beliefs, and ways of being in the world. This enables us to provide assignments and practice that connect both to the students' worlds and to the big ideas and key skills.

Practice needs to be linked to students' lives and their funds of knowledge. Practice needs to help bridge the gap between students' funds of knowledge and those funds of knowledge expected and required by the school and by standardized tests.

All students can experience a disconnect between their joy in learning outside school, on the basketball court or riding bikes or working on cars or playing electronic games or using the internet. Even low academic achievers learn and enjoy learning outside of school. Because they don't think of what they do outside school as learning, these students don't make the connection between learning outside school and learning in school.

Help students connect new knowledge with their existing knowledge—especially their cultural knowledge, experiences, and interests. Everything students already know and have already experienced is a resource for understanding what they are learning in school. The world of each student, regardless of background, is a resource for us to connect their interests to learning in school—if we can find out what those interests are.

1. Decide What Needs to Be Practiced

Anything that involves having students process big ideas or use key skills is practice—especially using skills such as analyzing, explaining, contrasting, and so on. It's for you to determine what students should be practicing and how often they should be practicing it. There's not enough time to practice everything—practice only what students aren't doing well on. Here are some questions you might ask:

- Based on your observation, what skills need practice, what big ideas need emphasis?
- How much time per week do students need to practice to learn a key skill they aren't doing well on? When can they practice?
- How can learners help one another practice (e.g., through activities in groups of two)?
- How will you monitor skill acquisition?

2. Have Students Practice Just Beyond Their Current Level of Mastery

Students who learn easily typically have high language skills, a large vocabulary, and a rich fund of knowledge that make them appear talented and intelligent. In contrast, students who don't have these skills don't appear intelligent and talented, when, in fact, they have not yet have acquired the skills and funds of knowledge they need to do well. For both groups, whatever skills they exhibit have mostly come from practice. We need to understand—and to help all students understand—that they have not acquired the knowledge and skills they need because they have not yet had enough practice.

In *Talent Is Overrated*, Geoffrey Colvin (2010) makes the point that students who appear talented have had more—and more effective—practice than those who appear untalented. Students who are better at taking tests have spent more time practicing—even if the practice didn't seem to them like practice. The way to master any skill is for students to always practice tasks that are a little beyond what they are capable of doing. There is no point to having students practice what they have already mastered; they need to be practicing what they have not yet mastered (Vygotsky, 1978).

Consider Ways to Differentiate Practice

Students need to practice what is a little beyond what they can do. Having students practice skills that are too far beyond what they're capable of doing leads to giving up or to failure. You probably don't need to create separate lessons for the highest and the lowest achievers, but you do need to find ways to differentiate practice. There are no easy ways to do this, but there are strategies that may apply to your situation:

- Having students tutor one another can be an effective way to have students practice at the appropriate level of difficulty. Tutoring has been shown to help both the tutor and the tutee.
- Having students working in heterogeneous groups has been shown to be effective in boosting the achievement level of all students.
- Designing assignments and projects where students can do the assignments at their own level increases agency and effective practice.

Give Low-Achieving Students Extra Practice

Working with parents to provide extra practice, giving extra credit, giving homework, and providing individual help before class are approaches teachers have used successfully.

Consider Using a Mastery Approach for Key Skills

A mastery approach is a way of differentiating learning that works well for learning skills. Students learn skills at different rates, so using a mastery approach can be a good option where sequential materials are readily available, such as in math, reading, spelling, and so on.

3. Schedule Distributed Practice

Most skills are best learned through distributed practice—that is, through many short periods that involve students in practicing behaviors that are slightly beyond their present level of mastery. Consider your experience with a coach, whether piano teacher, drama instructor, band director, or a sports coach. Your coach was there to critique your performance, to give advice, and especially to structure your activity, to give you short-term goals, and to keep you going despite discouragement. You did the work, but the coach broke down tasks (that would have otherwise been overwhelming) into activities you could succeed at. Practice sessions might have been long, but they were broken into short periods practicing different drills or other activities.

Keep in mind that distributed practice is not so much about how long practice sessions last, but how many days a week students need to practice a particular skill. For skills that involve memory or motor skills (such as spelling, arithmetic, keyboarding, playing a sport or a musical instrument) practicing a short time every day is much better than a longer time once a week. Students with more skill can profit from longer practice periods. Textbox 9.1 provides tips for scheduling practice.

TEXT BOX 9.1. TIPS FOR PRACTICE

- Schedule tasks that require more concentration earlier in the day.
- Keep periods of practice short. The harder the task, the shorter the practice period needs to be.
- For tasks needing distributed practice, use several shorter periods rather than one longer period. Ten or fifteen minutes per day will work better than a longer period once or twice a week.
- Provide variety. More difficult or more stressful tasks may require switching tasks frequently.
- Establish a routine. A specific time and a set order of tasks will save time and help put students in the frame of mind to learn.
- As a task is mastered, lengthen periods of practice. When longer periods become satisfying, do not arbitrarily cut off the activity or you will kill motivation.
- Use Premacking (see Chapter 7) and end each practice session with the most satisfying activity for the students.
- Wherever possible, help students see their practice as part of a pattern or strategy that they can use in similar situations.

Schedule Time for Summative Projects

You need longer blocks of time for summative projects that synthesize big ideas and key skills and require creativity and higher-order thinking. Summative projects are also important because they enable students to learn more complex skills while involving them in using (and therefore practicing) less complex skills. Make sure projects involve learning, practicing, and consolidating big ideas and key skills—and use scoring guides to measure this. Once students are involved in doing a project, don't pull them away to other tasks while they're still motivated and working productively. This kills their motivation and teaches them to avoid deep involvement because they'll be pulled away.

Summative projects often involve writing, and the next section provides writing guidelines.

GUIDELINES FOR WRITING

Guidelines for writing are divided into two parts: first drafts and revisions—including editing and proofreading.

Guidelines for Writing First Drafts

You can improve first drafts by providing structure. Use any of the following that make sense for your assignments.

Use Pump Primers

- Provide students with examples.
- Provide students a sentence stem to get them started.
- Give students a technique and show them a variety of examples, and have them create their own examples.

Draw It, Make a Diagram, Explain It

To make the task of beginning an assignment easier and more successful, have students:

- Make a drawing, diagram, word web, mind map, concept map, or outline
- Explain their idea and their graphic representation to a partner

Use Templates

Using a template repeatedly helps it become a habit—and a skill. A template can help students structure their revisions. For example:

- Steps for working a math word problem (Having students write their own math problems can give them insight into how such problems are put together, making it easier to understand such problems.)
- A lab report form on which students describe an experiment
- A book report form that guides students in describing and critiquing a book
- A template for writing a personal or business letter
- A template for a research paper

Have Students Double-Space Everything

Double-spaced material, whether typed or written, is easier to read and edit and is a courtesy to you, the teacher. Another advantage to double spacing is that it fills the page faster—an important point in making practice less intimidating.

Have Students Cross Out Instead of Erasing

When students practice writing, have them write in pen and cross out instead of erasing. Crossing out saves time and focuses on revising instead of on having a good-looking draft. Consider having students use pen because pen is usually easier to read. Do not ask students to redo work for minor errors; as students write more and then later revise, spelling and grammar will improve. The goal is to avoid making writing a hated task. Once a student hates to write, the chances of improvement are remote.

Guidelines for Revision, Editing, and Proofreading

Editing, rewriting, and proofreading help move students beyond their current level of skill in both writing and reading (e.g., writing complex sentences has been shown to help students improve reading comprehension of complex sentences).

Have Students Proofread in Groups of Two or Three

It's much easier to proofread someone else's papers than your own—and to do a better job. Having each student proofread one or two other students' papers gives everyone practice in proofreading—and this is a good way to learn to proofread with a minimum of pain. Some students will not be good proofreaders, so you may want to create groups of three where at least two members are adequate proofreaders, ensuring that each paper receives adequate proofreading.

If you are using computers, you can allow students to use spellcheckers, but have the computers set so that words are not corrected automatically, as this leads to errors and doesn't give students practice deciding how a mistake should be corrected. Proofreading is still necessary. As we know, spellcheckers don't catch mistaken words, only misspelled words.

Have Students Silently Move Their Lips and Vocal Cords—or Read Aloud

Proofreaders (including adults) need to slow themselves down enough to catch mistakes and the best way to do this is to read aloud very quietly or silently but moving one's lips. Sure, moving lips is not the sign of a good reader, but they are not trying to read; they are trying to proofread. Good readers have trouble catching mistakes because they see whole words and phrases at a time, not individual letters.

Some students will resist reading aloud or reading silently while moving their lips, so if you want them to do it you will need to walk everyone through the procedure simultaneously. For example, you can pass out a paper to be proofread, then you can have everyone read along with you, first aloud, and then silently but still moving your lips. Students learn what the teacher has them do, not what the teacher says to do.

WRITING IN PASSES: A PROCEDURE FOR WRITING

Writing in passes is a way to combine all the above guidelines into a procedure you can use over and over. Many students get stuck when called on to write because they try to write, correct mistakes, and evaluate all at once. In the long run, students will do better work by working through a project in a series of separate passes where one thing is completed on each pass. The idea of working in passes can be used by third-graders writing a story, by high school students doing a report, or by teachers completing a graduate portfolio.

By providing more structure to writing assignments, you provide more support. The steps below provide one approach to having students practice revising. Modify the steps to fit your situation. The key idea is to walk students through each step. Walk around and make sure that students are doing what you ask so that you can help those students who are stuck.

Pass 1. Brainstorm and Write Down the Idea

After you've given a prompt, have students come up with an idea and ask them to describe the idea. The description could be a paragraph, concept map, diagram, drawing, or a worksheet asking for details about the idea. You can substitute freewriting or have students explain their idea to a partner. Have students do this quickly, in no more than five or ten minutes. Consider having students brainstorm in teams of two (see Chapters 10 and 11 on team learning).

Pass 2. Write an Outline

Making outlines is difficult for many students. You can provide verbal prompts (or a worksheet) that walks them through a series of questions such as What's the first thing you want to talk about in your paper/story? What comes next? What comes after that? If students have done a concept map or a list of ideas, they can simply number the ideas in the order they want to write about. Have students edit, cut, and paste as necessary. The point of these first two passes is to help students create a structured plan.

Pass 3. Write a Rough Draft

If the first two passes have been thoroughly done, the rough draft will almost write itself. Do not evaluate misspelling or other errors until after the very last pass. Make it clear that you do not expect or even want mistakes corrected on the first drafts.

Have students read their drafts to one another in pairs or have students exchange papers and edit one another's papers—whatever is appropriate for your students. Then have students make corrections on the rough draft.

Pass 4. Put Aside for a Day or More, Then Rewrite

Wait at least one day between drafts. Students need to feel good about what they've written—and to get some distance before revising.

Pass 5. Make a Final Draft

Have students make a final draft, proofread it, and hand in the final draft.

GUIDELINES FOR WORKING IN PASSES

Make each pass a separate project to be discussed and evaluated, and celebrated when that pass is complete. If students still hand in a paper that is of poor quality, have them do additional passes. If the project is difficult, they may do some passes many times, but even when this is necessary, make each pass as easy and relaxed as possible. Consider the following:

- Limit the amount of time for each pass.
- After each pass, stop, take a break, and share feelings about how that pass went.
- Modify the procedure to fit your situation—you don't want to make the process overly difficult or even painful (which you can know by observing students' verbal and non-verbal behavior).

USE THE PASS METHOD FOR NONWRITING PROJECTS

The pass method can also be used for projects and performances that are not writing or are not only writing, such as:

- Doing math problems and checking them at a later time (or checking another student's work),
- Giving a presentation,
- Making a map,
- Making concept maps that explain an event or a process (e.g., the branches of government or organization of a corporation),
- Preparing a play.

A SCRAP OF CONVERSATION

My task as a counselor was often to get students working again. Sometimes a student just didn't know what to do—that is, she knew what to do, but not how to do it. The teacher would ask for a paragraph and she would write a sentence. We would have a conversation: "Tell me more about this story of yours." And she did, and I would have her write down what she just said, and she was done. Here's a simple procedure to generate a paragraph: Have students tell someone about their day, their story, their dog, whatever they're supposed to write about. Procedures, in other words, don't have to be complicated. The hard part can be figuring out what procedures are needed. Not everyone in class may need the procedure, but everyone can profit from using it.

As for me, I love doing the first draft and hate doing the revisions—dozens, in the case of this book. But revision is what it takes to get things right—and it builds skills of all kinds. When our son objected to revising a paper because his sentences wandered up and down the page, sometimes even crossing, he said in his defense: "The teacher didn't say we had to write on the lines." After he recopied his work a few times, the problem disappeared. And he was a middle-schooler! Revision not only allows all students to improve, it also helps them figure out what they want to say and then say it.

CONCLUSION

Changing to a practice-based approach is a way to involve students in learning big ideas and developing key skills by actively using them. Even in seemingly information-based subjects such as history, literature, and science, the ability of students to understand the big ideas in that content is based on practice—whether that practice consists of reading, writing, or speaking.

For students who come to class with a deep fund of knowledge and sophisticated written and oral language skills, reading and listening may be enough to learn. For those students who lack these skills, extensive practice needs to be included—and extensive practice will also boost the understanding and skill of those already operating at a high level. Students catch on very quickly to where quality doesn't matter, and then they won't bother doing quality work. Revision is a way to create quality work.

Q & A

Q. *Isn't practice just another name for repetition?*
A. Mindless repetition is rightly criticized. On the other hand, you learn how to become good with a hammer by doing a lot of nailing. Mindless? Try using a hammer without paying attention—your thumbs will be all bandages in a very short time! If only all forms of learning involved such direct feedback.

Q. *Most of what I teach involves reading and understanding. Little or no practice is required.*
A. Learning anything involves a skill. Reading, listening, writing, speaking, describing, explaining, analyzing, and the like don't involve a lot of drill, but they do require practice. We don't always think of what learners do as

practice. If you enjoy reading history, you don't think of the reading you do as practice; you're just reading history—easily, fluently, and for pleasure. But of course, it's through reading a lot of history that one becomes fluent in history—and reading.

Q. Is there a problem with having students critique one another's work? What about confidentiality?

A. You are not asking students to grade one another's work and you are not sharing your grades, so confidentiality is not an issue. You do need to teach students to be helpful and kind!

ADDITIONAL RESOURCES

Berger, R. (2003). *An ethic of excellence*. Portsmouth, NH: Heinemann.

> A treasure trove of ideas and practices having to do with practice and revision. You don't have to teach like Ron Berger to use his ideas on multiple revisions (Berger's book is also mentioned as a resource in Chapter 6).

Colvin, G. (2010). *Talent is overrated: What really separates world-class performers from everybody else*. New York, NY: Portfolio Trade.

> An excellent treatment of what constitutes effective practice. Colvin also presents a convincing case that most of what we attribute to talent is a matter of extensive practice. Applied to school, his book suggests that doing well in school is related more to the skills and prior practice students bring to school than to talent or intelligence.

Wexler, N. (2019). *The knowledge gap: The hidden cause of America's broken educational system—and how to fix it*. New York, NY: Avery.

> The second half of Wexler's critique of schools is a review of research that shows, among other things, that writing and reading comprehension are related—providing another reason to have students actively engaged in writing.

Chapter Ten

Use Teams to Increase Practice

"If you want to change attitudes, start with a change in behavior."
—William Glasser

Teams provide a way for students to use their existing fund of knowledge and vocabulary to acquire and practice the fund of knowledge necessary for them to understand big ideas and practice key skills. Team learning is a huge topic. This chapter will get you started; the following chapter provides additional possibilities and guidelines for using team learning.

In well-managed team activities, students can increase both their skills and their understanding. Using team learning enables teachers to provide more practice time because students in small groups can be practicing skills simultaneously. Also, successfully managed team activities increase cooperation and community. This keeps students working, especially students from cultures who prefer cooperation over competition.

We know what doesn't work: putting students in groups and giving them a task without providing training in appropriate procedures or accountability. The secret to team learning is to prepare a procedure very thoroughly, then use that procedure over and over until it becomes so familiar that it becomes easy and efficient to use. At that point, your preparation gets easier and faster.

You get to know the procedure so well that you can begin to think of modifications in the process of planning or teaching. You also get to know the procedure so well that you can give students ten minutes to do a task and then, if you see that most of them are finished after six minutes, you can give them another minute, bring the activity to a close, and move on to the next thing.

Knowledge is not a thing that exists by itself, like a beach ball sitting on a beach waiting for someone to pick it up. Whether we're five or fifty-five, we create knowledge in ourselves by using language. We sometimes struggle to find the words to say what we think, and at the same time we discover what we think by finding the words that seem to fit what we're trying to say. This is the same process that happens when team learning is used to have students develop their understanding of big ideas by engaging in skills like describing and explaining.

BENEFITS OF TEAM LEARNING

Why don't teachers use team learning more? Without appropriate procedures, team learning can be frustrating and not very successful. To work, team learning needs to be well managed and provide a high level of individual accountability for all students. Using effective procedures to manage teams takes care of most of the objections to team learning, leaving the benefits. Let's look at some of these benefits.

Teams Can Increase Practice of Ideas and Skills

You can do simple cooperative activities in teams of two for one or two minutes at a time and you can incorporate these activities into presentations as a way of keeping students involved (more on this in Chapter 13). Short activities can keep students attentive, build skills, and prepare students for more complex team learning activities.

The ability to read and write formal language lags behind the development of oral language. Team learning provides the opportunity for language development and conversation that students need to succeed. Extensive practice in skills of speaking and listening, asking and answering questions, explaining, describing, and problem solving can build skills in students who need them while allowing students with extensive skills to enhance their skills.

One challenge when involving students in learning is that traditional methods of calling on students take too much time. Using teams of two in a class of twenty students can provide ten times as much practice answering questions as a teacher-centered class where students answer one at a time. Ten students in pairs can be sharing their answers at the same time with their partners versus one student responding to the teacher. When you consider that the person listening in a two-person team must also take responsibility for being a good listener, the amount of participation is even greater.

Teams Help Create a Learning Community

Team learning has been shown to work well with students from diverse populations, cultures, and family backgrounds (Kagan & Kagan, 2017). Students from cultures that value relationships over achievement may not be willing to work unless their needs for relationships and cooperation are met (Payne, 2005; Johnson, Johnson, & Holubec, 1994). Physical integration of diverse groups into the same class and the same school does not by itself produce acceptance or cooperation. Working in teams provides a way to integrate class members from diverse cultural, racial, and ethnic backgrounds into a class where everyone cooperates.

Team learning provides opportunities for all students to meet their needs for belonging when they cooperate with others, power when they succeed, fun when they work together, and freedom when they can make choices about what they are doing (Glasser, 1998b). Students who do well on their own can do just as well or better by doing some learning in teams.

Help students feel part of a team and you encourage a willingness to take responsibility and work harder. When we look back to our positive experiences of school, we tend to remember the experiences we had as a part of a group—the sports team, the band, the science club, the choir, the history class that re-enacted a Civil War battle. Team learning is an effective way to motivate students and involve them in learning (Kagan & Kagan, 2017; Glasser, 1998a; Johnson, Johnson, & Holubec, 1994, 2007).

Working in Teams Prepares Students for a Diverse Adult World

Since the beginning of the twentieth century, schools have experimented with group projects and other forms of team learning and have almost always pulled back—sometimes because of the difficulties involved, sometimes because of dissatisfaction with results, and sometimes because of an insistence on a "return to basics." This time, however, the movement toward team learning is different: We are now living in an increasingly diverse society where learning to work cooperatively has become a necessity.

The ability to work with others in teams is an essential adult skill. Preparing individuals to compete solely as individuals can be counterproductive. Students who work in teams learn cooperation and social skills as well as subject matter (Kagan & Kagan, 2017). While organizations may compete with one another, the ability to function successfully within an organization requires cooperation.

GUIDELINES FOR TEAMS

Team learning works best when you (1) train students to cooperate effectively and (2) make them accountable for a public product or performance. The guidelines below can help you with team procedures you are already using, with the four team procedures that follow these guidelines, and with other procedures you may learn from colleagues and conferences. (See also Kagan and Kagan's *Cooperative Learning* [2017].)

Start with Lower-Risk Activities

Get experience doing simple, lower-risk activities. By thinking about whether an activity is low, moderate, or high risk for you at your present level of expertise and comfort, you can decide what activities you are comfortable doing and what the students can handle. The following descriptions may help you decide whether to use an activity.

Low-Risk Team Activities

A low-risk activity is one that requires little or no additional training and responsibility beyond what the class has already done. Keep in mind that a complex activity may be low risk for an experienced teacher with a well-trained class, but high risk for a less experienced teacher with an untrained class.

Moderate-Risk Team Activities

A moderate-risk activity requires training for students in team-learning procedures. You may be able to incorporate the training into the activity itself to make it lower risk.

High-Risk Team Activities

A high-risk activity requires much additional training for students or much additional experience for you before you will be comfortable attempting it. You may have a wonderful idea which may work well toward the middle of the year but not at the beginning of the year.

Teach Procedures Separately From New or Complex Content

Combining new material with a new procedure can create confusion. Teach the procedure first using material with which students are already very familiar.

Set Up Teams

The goal is to set up teams that allow students to practice using key skills to learn big ideas, and to develop the ability to cooperate. Consider the following factors in setting up teams.

Team Size

Choose team size after you've decided what students are going to do. The size and composition of teams can make a big difference in team success or failure. Keep in mind:

- The larger the team, the less responsibility each person has.
- It is better to have a team that is too small rather than too big. In a group that is too small, individual members will have plenty of work to do, whereas, in a group that is too large, individual members will not have enough to do.

Teams of two allow half the class to be speaking at once. Teams of two members are quick to set up, flexible, and provide maximum responsibility and participation.

Teams of three work well if there is enough work for each member; they provide more variety of input than a group of two but can be a mistake if the task at hand requires only two members. Teams of three members are useful when you have three roles or tasks that need to be performed (e.g., a listener, a speaker, and an observer).

Teams of four have high flexibility. Teams of four can easily generate variety (e.g., many ideas, many examples, many points of view). Teams of four can be useful where a task is best done in teams of two; then the teams of two can join together to share and synthesize their work.

Teams of five or six can work well in situations where you want students to share or brainstorm ideas. Create temporary teams by combining two or three teams of two to share results.

Use Heterogeneous Groups for Most Tasks

You can allow students to work with partners of their choice some of the time, but the rest of the time you want to use teams to meet the two interlocking goals of helping all students succeed and of building community. Students can learn the most from one another when groups are mixed by ability and background. Mixed-ability grouping has been shown to be effective in raising the overall level of achievement (Kagan & Kagan, 2017). Mixed grouping by background has also been shown to be effective in developing acceptance and understanding of others from different backgrounds (Kagan & Kagan, 2017).

Structure Team Learning

Team learning can involve all students in using key skills to engage with big ideas. But using teams can be a waste of time unless you structure activities with the big ideas and key skills in mind—and build in accountability. One way to build in accountability is to always have students work toward creating a product or performance (more on this in the next chapter). Team learning should always include a product or performance because these create accountability. Creating a complex product or performance should require students to go beyond their current level of skill and understanding.

Specifying a product or performance may not be enough. It seems logical to put students in teams, give them an assignment, and hold the teams accountable, but without additional structure, some of the better students may take over and do all the work while other students do (and learn) very little. The following sections consider how to structure complex team learning in ways that bring all students up to a basic level while encouraging high ability students to also raise their level.

Differentiate Teams

There are two ways to deal with differentiation: You can give assignments where everyone can succeed at their own level or you can give individual students tasks that are appropriate for their level. The point to keep in mind about differentiation is that you only need to differentiate when students are not learning. Otherwise, diversify groups by ability and background.

Assign Students to Groups to Ensure Diversity and Avoid Conflict

Assigning groups has the advantage of giving the teacher total control to do what seems best—and the possible disadvantage of becoming the target of students who are unhappy in their groups. The older the students, the more they may resist this approach.

Arrange for All Students to Work With One Another

Over several weeks, arrange groups so that everyone works with everyone else. This can require an extra effort when you have students who don't get along. On the other hand, in the long run, building community can help the class function better.

FOUR TEAM PROCEDURES

The four procedures that follow provide an easy, low-risk way to get experience with team learning activities. Versions of these and many other procedures can be found in *Kagan Cooperative Learning* (Kagan & Kagan, 2017) and online. Additional team procedures can be found in the next chapter.

Team Learning Procedure 1. Write-Pair-Share

Write-pair-share is a flexible procedure that can be used for almost any topic that can be discussed in pairs. Having students write provides individual accountability; having the teams share with the whole class provides team accountability. Writing can be collected at the end of the exercise or at the end of the period.

Here is a four-step procedure for write-pair-share:

Step 1. Give students a question to answer in writing. Give them several minutes to write their individual answers.

Step 2. When students finish writing (or time is called), have them turn to a partner and share their answers. If students are in rows, you can alternate having students share with the person across from, in front of, or behind them. (The students left over if you have an odd number of rows can share with other people in their row. The students left over when students share with the person in back of or in front of them can share across rows.) If it bothers you to have students move their chairs (or if the chairs are bolted down), you can say, "Without moving where you are, form a group of two."

Step 3. Have each pair count off by twos (one, two) within their pairs. Have all the ones stand. (Alternate this with having the twos stand.)

Step 4. Have each person standing share a one-sentence conclusion with the whole class. Each person should sit down after sharing. If you use this procedure regularly, alternate who stands so that everyone has to stand up and deliver half the time, but no one will know whose turn it will be. Accountability is built into the structure.

How to Use Write-Pair-Share

You can use write-pair-share to review a previous lesson, to find out what students already know about a topic, to summarize a lesson, or to answer a question you pose. You can ask questions that allow you to informally assess what students are learning, such as:

- What is something you learned about... [identify specific topic]?
- What is something a teacher might ask about... [identify specific topic]?
- What is something a student might be confused about?

Variation of Write-Pair-Share

A variation of write-pair-share is to have two groups of two share their answers with each other. Have one person from the group of four share with the class.

Team Learning Procedure 2. Think-Pair-Share

Think-pair-share is a strategy developed by Frank Lyman (1987). This is the same procedure as write-pair-share, except instead of having students write, have them pair up, then discuss a question (without writing). After several minutes, call time, have students count off, and have half the students stand and share an answer. You can monitor the groups, listening in to see if students are learning. If the procedure is going well and you are short of time, you can ask for several volunteers to share (instead of having everyone share).

Team Learning Procedure 3. Sentence Completion

Sentence completion (Martin, 1980; Simon, Howe, & Kirschenbaum, 1995) can be done as a variation on write-pair-share or as a round-robin procedure (procedure 4, below). Give students a sentence stem and ask them to complete the sentence in writing or verbally, in a team of two, three, or four.

Step 1. Have students form groups of two (for example, "Without moving your chairs, form a group of two").
Step 2. Give students a question to answer or a statement to complete, such as:

- An example of [fill in topic] ...
- Something I just learned ...
- Something I liked about [fill in topic] was ...
- Something the British should have thought about when they wanted to expand their empire was ...
- An idea I found useful was ...

Team Learning Procedure 4. Round-Robin

Round-robin is a simple, low-risk procedure (Kagan and Kagan, 2017) that works well with small groups or with the whole class. Use whole class round-robin to teach the procedure, then use groups of four or five. This is effective as a closure activity or for reviewing test questions, asking for examples, having students read aloud, or brainstorming. Here is a three-step procedure for round-robin:

Step 1. Have the whole class or each group form a circle. If chairs are not movable, have students stand in a circle.
Step 2. Provide the class or group a question or statement to respond to.
Step 3. Going around the class or group, have each student answer in turn.

BUILDING EXPERTISE THROUGH PRACTICE

Both you and your students will gain expertise through practice of low-risk activities like the four presented in this chapter. After you and your students gain skill and confidence in working in groups, you can try more extended, more complex activities.

The secret to using team learning successfully is walking students through the procedures you want them to learn. As students learn what to expect and what to do, procedures become efficient and effective. The power of learning a procedure comes from having students use it repeatedly so that it becomes automatic—allowing teachers and students to concentrate on skills and content. Teach one and only one procedure at a time. Wait until the procedure has become automated for both you and the students before teaching another procedure.

The power of these procedures comes from using them regularly so that students become used to taking responsibility for what they are learning. Also, when you use these procedures regularly, they become a habit for both you and the students—allowing you to involve students in an efficient way that leads to greater understanding and retention. Having several procedures that work well is like having a cash reserve in your checking account.

A SCRAP OF CONVERSATION

I was not a team learner. Give me a book to read and I'll learn from it. In one of my education classes, I was assigned to a group for a group presentation. I'm still ashamed to say I didn't do my part. Yet I learned everything in this chapter in teams at workshops and conferences. I learned and enjoyed the process. That's how you do it. Get experience by sitting in on a class, or going to a conference or a workshop. Not as good, but still helpful: Go to youtube.com and type in "think-pair-share," "cooperative learning strategies," or similar phrases.

CONCLUSION

Team learning is an effective way to practice a variety of key skills to understand and manipulate big ideas. That's the main point. Higher-order key skills such as analyzing, synthesizing, evaluating, problem solving, and critical thinking are learned through conversation and writing as much or more than through listening and reading. Team learning enables students to understand challenging ideas and questions by talking and writing. High-stakes testing typically involves understanding challenging ideas and questions. More broadly, we construct our view of the world as much through conversation as we do through listening to presentations and reading textbooks.

Team learning is a method that has been shown to work with students from diverse backgrounds—some of whom will not learn from other methods until they feel they are part of the class. You don't need to write separate lesson plans for team learning and you can include a variety of teaching methods in the same period. The next chapter looks at the challenge of involving students in more complex team activities and projects.

Q & A

Q. *No one in my school uses team learning. Will this create a problem?*
A. Simple procedures—like write-pair-share, think-pair-share, sentence completion, and round-robin—are a good way to begin because they are very low key and students can do them at their desks. You can have students move without creating a problem as you gain skill and confidence.

Q. *Are there other seating arrangements you can suggest in addition to circle formations?*
A. You can have students face one another whether they're in groups of twos, threes, or fours. If you want them to work independently, the seating arrangement doesn't matter as long as they aren't disturbing one another. In the lower grades, groups of four desks can be set up so that students face each other as they would in a booth at a restaurant; that way you can have them work independently, or in pairs next to each other, pairs across from one another, or all four together. This flexibility can allow you to flow from one activity to another with almost no transition time. You can always try something knowing that if it doesn't work, you can change it.

ADDITIONAL RESOURCES

Kagan, S., & Kagan, M. (2017). *Kagan cooperative learning*. San Clemente, CA: Kagan.

The definitive work on procedures for team learning. An essential resource that provides step-by-step instructions for dozens of generic cooperative learning procedures, including procedures for developing class and team cooperation, building thinking skills, reviewing for tests, and problem solving.

Chapter Eleven

Plan Projects That Use Teams

> Already being used by thousands of teachers across North America, the learning-team model has been proved effective by years of extensive research.
>
> —William Glasser

Key skills such as explaining, analyzing, and problem solving are learned through writing and conversation as much as or more than by reading and listening. Team-learning projects can include more practice in writing and conversation because they allow multiple teams to function simultaneously (for example, see the Foxfire books, Wiggington, 1972, 1973, 1974). You can create an unlimited number of longer team-learning activities that involve teams in practicing key skills to process big ideas. This chapter focuses on projects taking more than fifteen minutes, including projects done over multiple class periods. It provides a project planning template and three examples for using the template, plus a final section on using the template in planning large projects.

TEAM PROJECT PLAN

Teams can be used to create team products and performances and can also be used to help revise and improve individual projects through activities such as using scoring guides (see Chapter 7), listening, asking questions, proofreading—or through combining individual contributions into a group product, such as a video, poster, or in-class magazine designed to meet curriculum goals.

Setting up team learning is like setting up a lesson plan, and you can use the same procedures over and over. There are many more team procedures you can find online or in Kagan and Kagan (2017). The approach in this chapter is to give you a project plan template that you can use to create your own plan.

The heart of the chapter is Table 11.1, *Team Project Plan Template*. A project plan can be contained in a single lesson or a series of lesson plans. Making a project plan is similar to making lesson plans (see Chapter 5). You can use the template and then roll it into your lesson plans.

Table 11.1. Team Project Plan Template

Big Ideas _____		
Key Skill(s) _____		
Product or Performance _____		
Time Allotted	Individual, Team, or Whole-Class Task	Activity

Step 1. Decide What Students Need to Practice

As developed in the previous chapter, team learning provides a way to have students use key skills like describing, explaining, analyzing, and so on to develop a deeper understanding of big ideas. Step 1 is to identify the skills students need to develop and the big ideas they need to understand more deeply and then to identify a product or performance that will demonstrate that students have learned these. Public products and performances are best because students typically care more about looking competent than they do about a grade. A public product or performance is also an excellent way to ensure accountability. "Public" can mean sharing with the whole class, putting up papers in the hallway, presenting to another class, and so on.

Step 2. Decide on Team Activities

The following tasks don't have to be done in order. Enter items on the template (Table 11.1) as they occur to you.

Task 1. List Activities

Enter activities students will need to do into the template. When you begin, it may be difficult to think of what activities are needed, but if you fill in items as you think of them, the assignment will begin to take shape.

Task 2. Decide Which Activities Are Individual, Team, and Whole-Class Activities

Deciding whether an activity is an individual, team, or whole-class activity is the only difference between the project plan template (Table 11.1) and the lesson plan template (Table 5.1). As you plan your project assignment, decide what will be individual activities students do on their own, what will be team activities, and what will be whole-class activities. (See Table 11.2, *Team Project Plan for Making Concept Maps: Short Version* for examples.) Use your best judgment to create and structure the activity.

Step 3. Decide on Time Blocks

Once you have decided on an activity, decide how much time you need for that activity. This gives greater control over the flow of the project—just as with the lesson plan template (Table 5.1 in Chapter 5). Simply fill in the amount of time needed for each task in the first column of the project template (Table 11.1).

THREE SAMPLE PROJECT PLANS

The best way to see how the team project template works is to look at examples.

Sample Project Plan 1. Making Concept Maps: Short Version

Concept maps can be a good project because they engage students in higher-order thinking that shows how big ideas relate to one another and to supporting ideas—an essential part of forming semantic memory. (*Semantic memory* refers to understanding and remembering material that is complex, nonlinear, cannot readily be put into story form, and benefits from graphic representation such as the water cycle.) The teacher could just pass out premade organizers, but students will not learn from them in the same way they will if they make their own.

The topic could be in any content area—science, history, government, literature, and so on. To ensure that students include all key terms, you can include a list of terms. Table 11.2 is a short version of a plan for having students make individual concept maps, revise in groups of two and share what was learned.

Concept maps tend to work better when you restrict the number of terms to somewhere in the neighborhood of four to six terms. Carefully monitor the maps to ensure they are correct; otherwise, students will learn incorrect information.

Table 11.2. Team Project Plan for Making Concept Maps: Short Version

Time Allotted	Individual, Team, or Whole-Class Activity	Activity: Concept Maps
10 minutes	Individual	Make individual concept maps using the following terms: [Provide a list of terms.]
10 minutes	Teams of Two	Exchange maps, write comments on the back of the map: Something I like about your map is . . . Something you could include in your map is . . .
5 minutes	Whole-Class	One person from each team shares what they learned.

Sample Project Plan 2. Making Concept Maps: Long Version

Table 11.3 provides a longer version of the plan illustrated in Table 11.2, in this case, having students make individual concept maps and then critique and revise them in groups. In a long version of making concept maps, you can have students add their own additional terms to the list you provide. The total allotted time of fifty minutes in Table 11.3 might not be enough or might be too much, depending on the complexity of the product required. The point of showing two different versions of the same basic plan is to show that you can modify any plan. Do whatever is appropriate. You have all the flexibility you need because you are in charge.

Sample Project Plan 3. Practice Review Test

Teams can be used to good effect for test review. Table 11.4 is an example of a summative plan for having students individually take a teacher-made multiple-choice test for review, then having the students get into teams and take the test as a group. Retaking the test as a team allows students to have conversations about the correct answers, which is practice not only in taking the review test but also in listening and verbalizing about the answers and why an answer is correct. You can then hand out the answer key and have students check their answers. The amount of time needed will change depending on how long the test is. Modify the plan to fit your situation.

Table 11.3. Team Project Plan for Making Concept Maps: Long Version

Time Allotted	Individual, Team, or Whole-Class Activity	Activity: Concept Maps
10 minutes	Individual	Make individual concept maps using the following terms: [Provide a list of terms.]
15 minutes	Team	Exchange and discuss concept maps, do peer critique of others' maps, write comments on the back of each map.
5 minutes	Individual	Everyone revises their own concept maps based on student and/or teacher feedback.
3 minutes	Whole-Class	Students post their concept maps around the room and stay standing by their own map.
10 minutes	Whole-Class	Students rotate around the room clockwise, looking at all the other concept maps. When students have rotated back to their own map, they sit down. Note: Students won't look at the other concept maps very hard unless given a task such as leaving on comment using a Post-It Note.
2 minutes	Teams of Two	Students share what they have learned.
5 minutes	Whole-Class	Sentence Completion: Something we learned . . .

Table 11.4. Team Project Plan: Practice Review Test

Time Allotted	Individual, Team, or Whole-Class Activity	Activity: Practice Test
10 minutes	Individual	Have students individually take a short test you have devised to get them to think about key concepts.
10 minutes	Team	Round-robin: Retake the test as a group; team members take turns giving the answer. Teams are encouraged to have conversations about the right answer for each question.
8 minutes	Whole-Class	The teacher reads the correct answers and answers any questions that arise.
2 minutes	Whole-Class	Closure: One person from each team stands. One at a time, students standing share something they learned.

EXPERIMENT WITH THE PROJECT PLAN

Experiment with different ways of using the project plan. The more experimenting you do, the better you will get at estimating what has value. The *Team Project Plan Template* structures your thinking, and with enough experience, you can vary your plans in many ways. Eventually, you may not need the template; you may be able to do the plan in your head.

LARGE PROJECTS AND DREAM PROJECTS

As human beings, we understand what we have made. We like making things and we learn from the activity. Build a tower, make a poster, cook an egg, or write a poem and you gain skill and understanding. Beginning as infants, we have a built-in desire to achieve competence—a desire that can be encouraged through the successful experience of creating products or performances. Large projects fit with this human desire to make things.

This section considers additional considerations and steps you need to take in planning a larger project. One suggestion is that if you have a very large project, consider getting experience by doing parts of the project.

Chapter 4 considered dreams and dream projects as part of your vision. You may not be able to do all the things that you want to do, but you can almost always do them in some form. The project template (Table 11.1) is very flexible and can be used both for short team learning activities and for large projects. Here are some examples based on the activities of actual teachers I heard speak at a National Science Teaching Association Conference:

- Peggy wants her students to make books to go into the school library. (She visited a school that did this.)
  What does making books have to do with learning big ideas and key skills? Everything. Making books creates connections with books and with school, with the teacher and with learning—and connections create caring about all of these. The contents of the books allow the writers to develop funds of knowledge and skills for developing ideas. Making books requires developing skills of writing, learning how to make paper, learning how to bind the pages, and so on. Making a book is a transformative process that students will remember all their lives and move them in the direction of being lifelong learners.
- Susanna wants to start a zoo in her classroom. (She met another teacher at a national convention who has already created a zoo at his school.)
  What does starting a zoo have to do with big ideas and key skills? This is a science teacher, so a zoo is relevant to the big ideas of biology. A zoo reflects everything that makes us care about animals. She can't have a zoo without student participation, which means the students need to learn everything they can about the animals so that they will be properly fed and cared for.

There are examples in every area. Teachers have done projects that involved staging a Civil War battle (history), writing and visiting elected government officials (social science), doing large design projects (art), staging an opera (music), and so on. Your idea can seem ridiculous, but you can always move in the direction of doing as much of it as is possible. Give yourself permission to think about what excites you and then incorporate those ideas into your designs for learning. What are your dream projects? What would you most like to do to make your classroom an exciting place for you and your students to be? Write down your answers. Begin to think about out how you can create projects and assignments that address your dreams and involve learning the big ideas and key skills.

Tie Dream Projects Into Big Ideas and Key Skills

We don't teach things just because we want to or because they've always been taught. We focus on the big ideas and key skills because that's our job and we want students to do well at the next level and on those high-stakes tests they must take. At the same time, school is not a factory and students are not products. The standards for each state (or the Common Core standards adopted by many states) are someone's best effort to define what students need to know to be successful and have a good life. The standards are imperfect, like the people who wrote them, but the standards exist for the sake of the human beings, not the human beings for the sake of the standards. We know these things, but when we're under pressure from all directions, it can be hard to remember.

Students can use funds of knowledge from their backgrounds as well as funds of knowledge that address the big ideas and key skills in the curricullum. The combination strengthens students' overall understanding and mastery because they are relating big ideas and key skills to their own backgrounds and funds of knowledge. Additional training or practice in needed funds of knowledge can be addressed through appropriate materials and practice. In other words, in the words of a multiracial psychiatrist friend, we are "one people, one planet." We might as well get good at it.

TASKS WHEN DOING LARGE PROJECTS

A large or very large project can follow the same basic steps presented earlier in the chapter, with some additions. You need to create a project prompt and a scoring guide before you start and revise as needed. The six steps presented here are reframed as *tasks* because you can do them in order, like steps. More likely, you will jump from one task to another as ideas occur to you—and that's fine. The three most important tasks in doing a project plan are to create a project prompt, a scoring guide, and a project plan. The likelihood is that all three will evolve together.

Task 1. Write a Project Prompt

A project prompt is likely to be the first thing you start and the last thing you finish. You may already have a project you've been wanting to try. It may be a project you saw a colleague doing, or a project you did before that you'd like to do again in a more structured way.

Task 2. Create a Scoring Guide

As soon as you have begun a prompt for your project, start a scoring guide. You're unlikely to finish either prompt or scoring guide before you finish your plan. You might even start with a scoring guide because a scoring guide requires you to be specific about what criteria you want the final product to meet. Creating a scoring guide will help you clarify what students are expected to learn and the evidence you expect to see. (Refer to Chapter 6 on scoring guides.)

Task 3. Make a Project Plan

Use the project plan template. You will probably need more blank lines than in the sample template. Don't worry if you don't think of everything all at once. It's going to take a week or so to figure out the details—and there will still be more details you haven't figured out. This is part of the process. Expect this to happen and it won't bother you.

Break the project into smaller chunks with deadlines for each chunk. Very likely, you'll need to make some adjustments as you go along.

Task 4. Set Up Teams

Use criteria from the previous chapter to set up teams that are heterogeneous by ability and background. You're asking students to make a commitment to the project, so you may want to give them some freedom to choose their teams. If you've spent the first several months using heterogeneous groups and the class has come together as a group, students will be more willing to work with one another and will have more experience doing so.

Give Students Some Choice

Anything that increases student agency can increase a sense of responsibility and reduce resistance to challenging assignments and projects. Give students a choice among topics (you still control what the choices are), a choice of when to present, and a choice of how much help they want from others or from you. Occasionally let students choose their own group, especially if you have been careful to use mixed-ability groups for shorter activities where students can get to know one another and can learn to work together. For projects, allowing students to choose their own groups can reduce resistance and increase cooperation, responsibility, and quality.

Task 5. Assemble Teams and Implement

This is the beginning of the project as far as the students are concerned. You will need to introduce the project over several days (or weeks) and give students time to think about what they would like to do. This calls for whole-class conversation (see the next chapter) where you discuss the project and bring students on board.

The bigger the project, the more likely it is that you will feel uncertain about how the project is going. Know that this is part of the process and then decide what comes next.

Task 6. Revise the Plan

As you make changes, keep notes on your project planning sheet. You may want to do the project again, and you will have forgotten all the changes and good ideas you came up with unless you write them down at the time.

BUILD EXPERTISE

There are many more procedures and many more principles that Kagan and Kagan (2017) and others have developed. The best way to learn how to do team learning is through participation. Go to a conference, workshop, or teacher development day that involves you in a team activity, then come back and try something you learned with your students.

Learning team procedures by doing them as an adult can convince you that doing a procedure the same way all the time every time does not create conformity or rigidity. It is an amazing thing to learn that as adults we are quite willing to be led through procedures, one step at a time. It is equally amazing to have the experience be both worthwhile and fun. Finally, it is amazing to realize that as we are learning through participation, that team learning is in many ways the same for kindergarten, elementary, and secondary students as it is for college and postgraduate students and other adults.

Get experience doing simple and intermediate team learning activities, and more complex activities will seem more doable, should you want to do them.

The video projects I saw students doing in New Franklin, Missouri were complex, but because students had years of experience with team learning and with taking individual responsibility, they had little difficulty in working productively—and the teachers were confident and relaxed.

A SCRAP OF CONVERSATION

A student complained on a student evaluation that he had learned a lot in my class, but he hadn't learned any of it from me. I told a teacher education professor friend and he laughed and laughed—because he didn't lecture; it was the students' job to come to class prepared and ask him questions. It took a while every semester, and students sometimes complained, but years afterward they would tell him how much they had learned. It takes effort to learn skills to do team learning, but with appropriate tasks and structure, everyone is engaged, everyone has something to contribute, and everyone can learn at their own level. And when students help one another, both sides learn.

Projects do work. A middle school teacher whose classes I visited taught by sharing with his students what they needed to learn, getting them on board, and having them create newsletters containing all the information they needed to know. When he was given warnings about the need to focus on covering all the material (instead of what he was doing), he wasn't intimidated. He reassured the administrator that his students' scores would be equal to or higher than other classes in the district. There are many ways to succeed, and his courage came from his confidence that he would succeed because he had succeeded many times.

Take a risk. It's easy to avoid starting something because you're not ready. Early in my career, one of my colleagues who came from a poor neighborhood in Boston was quizzing me on what I was doing. When I mentioned a project that I wanted to do but didn't feel ready, he gave me a piece of advice that has stuck with me year after year—advice that he himself had obviously taken. I'll always remember him saying, "If you wait 'til you're ready, you'll never do anything."

CONCLUSION

Until students have enough practice, team learning can be less productive than you would like. The secret is to start with simple procedures and use them over and over until students can do them. Then, while continuing to use the first procedure, teach a new procedure and practice that until students can use it efficiently and productively. By doing this, you will maintain control of your classroom, and you and your students will gain expertise in doing team learning. In particular, the simpler procedures like think-pair-share and write-pair-share can be incorporated into the flow of existing lessons (see previous chapter).

Be courageous: If you wait until you're ready to do team learning, you may never do it. Short, structured activities make it possible to learn how to do team learning in easy steps. Look for opportunities to provide more practice in using key skills and developing a deeper understanding of big ideas.

Q & A

Q. *I tried using team projects and students would argue. What do I do?*
A. Any time two or more people work together there will be different viewpoints because everyone has his or her own viewpoint. Conflict itself is not a problem; the problem comes when a lack of social skills and team cohesion leads to aggressive words or actions. When this happens, spend more time teaching procedures for building communication skills. *Kagan Cooperative Learning* (Kagan & Kagan, 2017) does an excellent job of providing strategies for doing this. The conflict can actually be very productive when students think about, analyze, and compare their different views—skills that are necessary to do well on high-stakes testing.

Q. *I did not like group work because I always ended up doing the work because I wanted a good grade. Other students freeloaded and still got the same grade I did!*
A. Successful approaches to team learning need to have both individual accountability and group accountability. If there is no individual accountability, individual students can goof off without consequence—an invitation some students will cheerfully accept! If there is no group accountability, students may do only what they need to do to get a good grade for themselves.

ADDITIONAL RESOURCES

Glasser, W. (1998a). *Choice theory in the classroom* (Rev. ed.). New York, NY: Harper Perennial.

An excellent introduction to choice theory, and how to use team learning, combined with Glasser's ideas on understanding and using students' internal motivation and Johnson, Johnson, and Holubec's (1994, 2007) approach to team learning.

Chapter Twelve

Use Conversation to Increase Learning and Build Community

"Before being allowed to enter the profession, prospective teachers should be asked to talk with a group of friendly students for at least half an hour and be able to engage them in an interesting conversation about any subject the prospective teacher wants to talk about."

—William Glasser

Having conversations is a theme that has run through the book. Getting to know students (Chapter 2) and helping them make choices (Chapter 3) involves conversation, however short. Engaging students in using scoring guides (Chapter 6), doing quality work, and making revisions (Chapter 9) all involve conversations. Increasing an understanding of big ideas through practice (Chapters 9, 10, and 11) involves conversation. Chapter 13 focuses on giving presentations that involve students by engaging them and each other in conversations. This chapter tackles questions regarding using conversation not otherwise considered.

WHY USE CONVERSATION

Conversations build vocabulary, funds of knowledge, language skills, and the ability to think—all of which are necessary for building reading and writing skills. Especially when working with students who lack these skills at the level necessary to do well in your class, conversation is essential in building them. The following sections consider the rationale for conversation in more detail.

Students Should Be Silent

A superintendent, in the act of criticizing a teacher who had middle school students moving around as they engaged in a biology lab, was heard to say, "If students are quiet and in their seats, they're learning." However much we disapprove of this superintendent's attitude and knowledge of learning, we all have our own interior censor that chides us if students are talking. And this censor is correct if students are not engaged in learning.

We've all pretty much grown up with the conviction that students do not need to talk and that even conversations that involve learning are enrichment and not essential. Let us look one more time at why conversation is essential for all students, especially those who have not yet acquired the vocabularies and funds of knowledge they need to do well in school (Schwandt, 1994; Solomon, 2000; Geert & Volman, 2004).

Conversation Builds Funds of Knowledge That Enable Reading and Writing

We learn to understand big ideas by reading, writing, listening, and talking about them. We can listen to what we already understand, but we get confused or misled when we listen to something we don't understand. Listening to presentations on big ideas is not enough to understand them unless students already have enough prior knowledge to grasp them. Otherwise, the experience is like those of us who are not in physics listening to a lecture on quantum mechanics. We hear and understand the individual words, but we can't understand the meaning from what we hear.

Skill in written language follows skill in verbal language. Appropriately structured conversation can help build verbal skill. In addition, in order to read material in a deep way (and do well on high-stakes tests) students need to build skills in describing, explaining, analyzing, and synthesizing that material—skills they can build through conversation.

Funds of Knowledge

Students all have their own funds of knowledge based on their experience and backgrounds. However, if, for whatever reasons, some students do not have the funds of knowledge, vocabularies, and language to understand and do well in school and on standardized tests, we need to help them acquire these funds of knowledge, vocabularies, and language. This is a problem in many countries, and at all levels, including universities.

In South Africa, Philip Baron has written about how the engineering curriculum of his university—using standard curricula used in European universities—makes assumptions about funds of knowledge, vocabularies, and language, including familiarity with examples his native South African students do not have. Yet, by getting to know his students, he can use examples and assignments that enable his students to succeed in meeting the stringent requirements for a university degree in engineering (Baron, 2018; Martin, 2018).

The differences in achievement among young children are relatively small; the farther in school students go, the larger are the differences at each subsequent grade level. There are huge differences among high school students where there were only small differences when they started elementary school. The conclusion is that it's never too late to start, but the earlier we start, the better and more easily we can help students who, for whatever reasons, do not have the funds of knowledge, vocabularies, and language skills they need.

Incorporating whole-class and small-group conversation within a lesson can be a powerful way to connect with students and to involve them in working not only on specific content skills and ideas, but also general academic language skills, problem-solving skills, and learning skills, as well as experiencing learning as a valuable activity (Barkley, Cross, & Major, 2005).

The Necessity of Conversation

The arguments for conversation and the techniques for carrying it out have been well known for at least the last half-century. Jean Piaget (Piaget, 1973, 1975; Kamii & Ewing, 2012) and Lev Vygotsky (1986, 1978), the two major developmental theorists of our time, both emphasize the importance of conversation in developmental learning. William Glasser (1975, 1998a, 1998b), and before him Rudolf Dreikurs (1968, 1991, 2012), devoted much of their careers to going around the country demonstrating and training teachers and parents in how to talk with students.

When teachers and administrators don't understand the necessity of conversation for students who come to school without knowledge and skills they need to succeed, conversation loses out to the demand for spending more time on using other methods. We will only use a method if we see that it's necessary (though we may use methods we're expected to use even if they don't work).

Conversations always involve thinking and learning on both sides. You learn what students are thinking, what interests them, what motivates them, what they understand, why they tried extra hard or why they gave up, and so on. You are then better able to connect with students and plan lessons that engage them in learning. You don't need to set aside a special time for conversation. Conversations don't have to be long; they can happen in the ordinary course of teaching.

Whether in small groups (as in team learning) or in whole-class conversations, the end goal is not to replace reading and writing with conversation but to prepare students for reading and writing. There's no point in having students answer questions at the end of the chapter if they don't read the chapter but immediately go to the back of the chapter, read a question, search for key words and phrases that address the question, then go on to the next question. This sort of chug and plug is a waste of time.

GUIDELINES FOR CONVERSATION

The topic of procedures once again arises as a way to provide structure. You learn how to structure and lead conversations by practicing, experimenting, taking risks, and making mistakes. Many teachers who try to allow more freedom in their classes close the door when they find that students do not know how to respond. You have to teach students to discuss without controlling what they say. When a class finally establishes a sense of group, the change may seem instantaneous, but the process of reaching this goal can be long and difficult. Even adult groups need structure to work. Without structure you can have a chaotic situation.

There are innumerable ways to conduct conversations. The advantage of the suggestions below is that they are procedures that, through repeated practice, become habits, allowing deeper learning. To have successful class conversations, all students need to be prepared and have something to say.

Ensure That Students Prepare

When students aren't prepared, conversation is usually, though not always, a waste of time. Class conversation often works better as a summative activity precisely because students are prepared. Consider having students write on their own and/or meet in small groups to address a question or problem and then discuss it in the larger class. Write-pair-share tends to work because students have prepared something to share. Sentence completion and other round-robin activities tend to work well as summative or review activities. Use conversation at the conclusion of having students using scoring guides when students have something to say.

Control the Process, Not the Conversation

You can control the process; you can't control what students say. Attempts to steer conversation according to a plan seldom work. If you try to force conversation, students will clam up, and then you are stuck. On the other hand, when you begin to see that you really cannot control what happens, you are in a much better position to relax and trust the group. Stay in control of the process by using procedures that work for you. That's one of the purposes of team-learning procedures. As soon as students begin to stray from the procedures you have set up, bring them back to the task or move on to the next task.

Develop a Few Simple Procedures for Conversations

Class members should discuss and help decide what the procedures will be. The procedures may be little more than a formalization of common courtesy that everyone knows (such as, *one person talks at a time*), but having students suggest them, making them into a rule, and then posting them in a prominent place puts the emphasis on following a structure rather than on the teacher having to take charge (Martin, 1980).

Have a Rule of No Criticism

Nothing kills problem solving and creativity faster than when class members make fun of or criticize others' ideas. Even if a student makes a suggestion intended to be humorous or disruptive, accept the idea and move on. Group members are more willing to talk when they know that those who disagree will say, "I see it this way . . ." instead of, "How can you say that?" (Martin, 1980). Asking students how they feel about criticism and how to solve the problem of criticism is better than laying down a rule. When the rule comes from the students, they will better understand and better follow the rule because they have been engaged in actively thinking, analyzing, and making conclusions. Of course, these are some of the same skills required in analyzing and making conclusions about the big ideas they're trying to learn. We learn to think by using language, so thinking about real situations and problems is relevant to developing needed skills.

Sit in a Circle

How do you get students to talk to one another? Having the class sit in a circle encourages students to interact more freely (Dreikurs, Grunwald, & Pepper, 1998; Glasser, 1969). Consider the following (quoted from Martin, 1980):

- A circle allows group members to see and be seen, to hear and be heard.
- In a circle, the teacher may still be a center of attention, but the teacher is in a much better position to allow others to be the center of attention when

they speak. One measure of a successful group is the extent to which group members talk with one another and to the group rather than addressing themselves to the teacher.
- In a circle, everyone is exposed; no one can hide behind furniture or other students. At first, this may be threatening, but when students who feel threatened find that they are accepted and not put down, they will be more willing to participate.

Give Students the "Right to Pass"

Allow students who don't want to speak to pass (Simon, Howe, & Kirschenbaum, 1995; Brookfield, 2006). "It is unethical to coerce students into talking about or sharing anything they do not want to" (Martin, 1980, p. 152). We have all been in groups where everyone was expected to "produce," and we strongly resented it. The right to pass encourages participation. By saying, "I pass," students are still participating. Saying, "I pass" involves at least a minimal commitment to the group, and it tends to draw that person into the group.

Build in Sufficient but Limited Time

Allow enough time for conversations, but try to schedule them at a time when there are built-in limits such as before lunch, the end of a period, or the end of the school day. If you find it hard to build in enough time for conversation (however short), keep in mind that in the long run, you will save time if the class learns to work together, to accept responsibility, and to do quality work.

Use Student Recorders

If you're solving a problem, have a student recorder write student suggestions on the board. If you're reviewing big ideas, have a student recorder write student contributions. If students are brainstorming, have a student recorder write down ideas as they are mentioned. Students can use whatever you have available—whiteboard, chalkboard, SMART Board, poster sheets. Having a student record contributions is a form of instant review and enables the other students to pay attention and reflect on what's being recorded, and lets you clarify or emphasize important points.

Discourage Monopolizing

When three or four students monopolize a class conversation, the conversation loses its value. If you find that you have a few students who dominate class discussions, here are some techniques to reduce monopolizing (from Martin, 1980):

1. Have a rule that a student who has spoken cannot speak again until everyone else has spoken. This is highly artificial, but it does work.
2. Turn problems back to the group: "It seems we have a problem—a lot of people are not talking at all. How do you feel about that?"
3. When students who do not usually talk look like they want to say something, invite them to speak: "Sarah, you look like you have some strong feelings about that." "Sarah?" may do just as well as an invitation to speak.
4. Ask individual students to monitor their own talking. (This is an option you might want to use only if your other efforts have failed.)

USE CONVERSATION TO AUGMENT DIRECT INSTRUCTION

Direct instruction (see Chapter 13) can include whole-class and small-group conversation to involve students in processing facts, ideas, and skills that the teacher is presenting.

Use Content Conversations to Involve Students

Subject matter class conversation is one way to involve students in higher-order thinking (Martin, 1980). The teacher provides expertise and guidance, leads conversations, and challenges students to think (Duffy & Cunningham, 1996).

Getting a group to talk—especially a large group of twenty or thirty or more—can be difficult. The most common reasons students give for not participating are that they do not have anything to say or they are afraid of looking foolish. In other words, they feel self-conscious. When students (or teachers) feel they are part of a group, they are less self-conscious about speaking. "Willingness to think, to challenge and be challenged, and to evaluate ideas is much more likely to take place where [students] feel acceptance and belonging" (Martin, 1980, p. 154).

Subject matter conversations should be used only when students have prepared. Use subject matter conversations as a summative activity after a quiz, a short paper, or other activity that involves students in processing materials. If students aren't prepared, the conversation will have little value.

Use Small Groups to Prepare Whole-Class Conversation

How do you get shy students to speak? Assign shy students to the same group and they are more likely to participate. Introverts don't like to speak spontaneously but are often willing to speak if they can prepare what they are going to say. Students who feel nervous about speaking in a large group will often talk in small groups, especially groups of two or three where everyone has a task, such as in think-pair-share.

Having students get to know everyone in the class through small-group conversation (or working in teams) prepares students to participate in a large-group conversation in several ways:

- As they get to know the other members of the class, talking to the class as a whole is less threatening.
- When students practice listening and conversation skills in small groups, they have better skills for large group conversations.
- When students work on specific tasks in small groups, they are much better prepared to share their ideas, findings, or conclusions with the class.

Use Sharing Conversations to Connect with Students

Sharing conversations help create a sense of community and get students to listen to and think about diverse ways of thinking (Au, 1998; Martin, 1980). They are not intended to solve problems, and no evaluations are made. Sharing conversations emphasize listening (Brookfield, 1991). Topics might include any topic relevant to the age and grade group you are working with. Topics can be relevant to subject matter, but they don't always have to be. Topics that meet the needs of students build a sense of community and make it easier to involve students in subject matter conversations (Schwandt, 1994; Spivey, 1997).

While conversations on matters of interest to students may not be directly related to content, they have value in the following ways:

- Any conversation in which students participate in a meaningful way involves them in thinking, listening, reflecting, and learning.
- Any genuine conversation involves its participants in exploring, analyzing, and higher-order thinking.
- Students may need to talk about events that affect them. The event could be a pleasant one, such as homecoming or the beginning of vacation, or it could be a tragic situation.

Use a Closure Activity

Closure is important—consider it a form of practice where students review what was just learned or decided. If there is enough time, invite everyone to share a phrase or a sentence. If time is short, ask two or three students to share a sentence. This is a good time to use a sentence completion procedure (see Chapter 10, Procedure 3), such as "Something I learned was . . ." using the round-robin structure.

A SCRAP OF CONVERSATION

I was the guest of a sixth-grade teacher who skillfully led a short conversation every morning, first thing, with the class. The floor was carpeted; teacher and students sat on the floor in a circle. Students could share whatever they liked—usually something that was going on in their lives. Sometimes there would be silence for what seemed like a long time, probably no more than ten or twenty seconds. The teacher was always calm, waiting for whoever decided to go next. The meetings didn't solve the problems her students had outside school, but they enabled the students to feel safe and ready to learn. The experience was striking, and I still remember her name forty years later.

CONCLUSION

Ability to read and to write almost always lags behind ability to use verbal language. Conversation can provide practice in using the vocabularies and funds of knowledge needed to understand and express big ideas. Conversation can also build a learning community characterized by motivation, ownership, tolerance, and cooperation.

Q & A

Q. *How do I learn to do group discussion?*
A. William Glasser, the founder of reality therapy and choice theory, put it best in workshops where my recollection is that he would say that he did group discussions over and over, and he learned how. The expert becomes the expert by doing.

Q. *I ask questions and everyone just sits there. What do I do?*
A. Older students (starting in middle school) don't like to take a chance that they'll be embarrassed. Try the write-pair-share strategy (Chapter 10): Have them write, then share what they've written with a partner, then ask for volunteers or call on individuals to share their answers. This way you get everyone involved and over a period or two you also end up calling on everyone.

ADDITIONAL RESOURCES

Simon, S., Howe, L., & Kirschenbaum, H. (1995). *Values clarification* (Rev. ed.). New York, NY: Grand Central Books.

A classic book of short activities you can use to encourage students to think about what is important to them and that can be used to engage students in short conversations with the whole class or with one another in groups of two or more.

Chapter Thirteen

Involve Students in Your Presentations

"Give a burst of information for ten minutes, then have them do something."

—Advice from a supervisor of adult education

When we present, we want students to pay attention and to actively process what we're saying. Create involvement and accountability and you can achieve this. Direct instruction refers to a method of teacher-guided learning that uses presentation, practice, and assessment. Direct instruction is sometimes reduced to teacher presentation, but direct instruction calls for providing information (including models and demonstrations), practice, and assessment to determine what students are understanding.

Direct instruction is most easily understood in the context of learning mathematics, foreign languages, and physical skills required in individual and team sports. In these areas, ideas and skills are inseparable. When we think of practice, we are likely to think of the type of practice involved in learning math, foreign language, or sports. What constitutes practice of other subjects is less obvious. A theme of this book has been that whenever students are using key skills to process big ideas, they are simultaneously practicing the skills and developing understanding of the ideas. More precisely, they are using the skills (such as describing, explaining, and analyzing) to understand the ideas more deeply, and through this form of practice they are both improving their skills and deepening their understanding.

Direct instruction is guided instruction. When you present, you have an opportunity to involve students in listening and seeing and then to have them clarify and solidify what they understand through answering questions, taking notes, taking quizzes, and asking questions. Going back and forth between making a presentation and checking for understanding provides a way to keep students engaged in both the presentation and the activities that check for and solidify understanding.

ORGANIZE MATERIAL TO FACILITATE UNDERSTANDING

Direct instruction (presentation combined with practice and on-the-spot assessment) can be effective only when the material is appropriately organized. The frequently heard criticism "knows the material but can't teach it" is one way of characterizing presentations that present the information but not in an organized way that can be absorbed into semantic memory.

Semantic Memory

Teaching the network of concepts that make up a big idea does not work if you give students all the information but it's not organized so that they can incorporate it into semantic memory—memory that incorporates material into a meaningful schema. Semantic memory is required for any interrelated network of concepts. Math and science are prime examples of information that needs to be carefully organized so that students can understand and retain them in semantic memory.

Use Semantic Organizers

Especially when knowledge is complex, how much students can learn from direct instruction depends on how well the information is organized and how much time students spend processing the information. The periodic table of elements, a taxonomy of animals, or a graphic representation of the branches of the federal government are all examples of schemas that can be understood and retained in semantic memory. They are also examples of semantic organizers—ways of organizing material that reveal the organization of the network of concepts that make up a big idea. That obviously doesn't mean that students will be able to reproduce structures like the periodic table of elements from memory (although they might be able to reproduce portions of them). What it does mean is that these graphic structures provide a way for teachers and students to consider information and show how it is related to other information in an organized way.

Unfortunately, most material cannot be organized so elegantly—which means you need to work hard to organize your presentations so that students can follow them. Students can then create their own ways of organizing the network of concepts you've presented so that they can retain them. Semantic organization in learning is a vast topic, but you can get a quick overview and examples by typing "semantic organization" into your browser.

WAYS TO ENCOURAGE STUDENTS TO PAY ATTENTION

The following principles can be used to keep students paying attention so that they can get the most from your presentations.

Keep Presentations Short

Divide presentations into short bursts of information (ten minutes) interspersed with student involvement. Few learners can digest and make sense of large amounts of information unless they have extensive, relevant prior learning.

Focus on Main Points and Relate Them to Prior Learning

Human beings of all ages retain more when presenters limit themselves to one or two big ideas and then tie everything else to those big ideas.

Use Advance Organizers

Students understand and retain more when presented material is organized so that the structure of the material is clear to them, so use advance organizers. An advance organizer can be anything that helps learners understand the structure of what they are going to learn and that they can tie to their prior learning. Letting students know the objectives of the lesson (mandated by some school districts) is an example. Providing students with semantic organizers (lists, outlines, diagrams, etc.) is another example.

An advance organizer can share the big ideas and key skills. You can let students in on what you are supposed to be teaching—and they are supposed to be learning—at the beginning of a unit, and you can ask them to help figure out the best way to learn the big ideas and key skills. This is an extension of letting students know the goals (objectives) of each lesson.

Define Concepts and Use Examples Relevant to the Students

Defining concepts and showing how they relate to one another is especially important for students who do not yet have the experience and background knowledge they need to understand the vocabulary you are using. Examples need to be relevant to the culture and experience of your students. Connecting with your students by getting to know them helps you know how to involve them through relevant examples. If you don't know what examples might be relevant, ask.

Help students follow a presentation by being very clear what the big ideas are and then showing how the material is related to the big ideas. Use diagrams, concept maps, timelines, and other graphic organizers to help students understand and retain the structure of the material. Have students explain how concepts are related, verbally and in writing, and have them practice making their own concept maps.

Use Story Form

Human beings follow and remember stories. Even in math and science, putting sequential information into story form can help students make sense of—and remember—sequential information.

WAYS TO INVOLVE STUDENTS

There are many ways to involve students which break up large blocks of information that would otherwise be indigestible for many students. Here are some ways.

Ask Rather Than Tell

We process questions differently than statements. Typically, we take in statements passively; questions, on the other hand, invite us to think of an answer. We are more likely to create and retain meaning when we come up with our own answers (Mooney, 2013).

Err on the side of asking questions rather than telling what you know. Asking a question prompts students to listen and to think of an answer. Until it becomes a habit, look for opportunities to ask questions. For example, ask students what they know about a topic, a concept, a vocabulary word, or an example. Ask for predictions instead of giving them, ask for reasons instead of giving them, or ask for closure statements instead of giving them. If you consistently err on the side of asking questions rather than telling, you will find out how much they already know as well as what they are understanding and where they are going astray.

Ask Open-Ended Questions

Open-ended questions allow learners to access their schema rather than trying to guess the answer you have in mind:

- Why did the main character leave home?
- How did you get your answer?
- Why did Lincoln issue the Emancipation Proclamation?
- What is something that you will take away with you from reading the story?

Ask for Examples

- Where have you seen an example of _____?

Use Closure Questions

Lesson closure doesn't have to come from the teacher; it can come from the students. For example:

- What is something you learned today about X?
- What one thing will you remember from the video we saw today?

Use Wait Time When Asking a Question

The average time a teacher waits for a response is on the order of one second. If students do not reply immediately, many teachers repeat, rephrase, ask a different question, or call on another student. Wait three to five seconds before you speak again, and the quantity and quality of responses will increase (Rowe, 1974). It's difficult to wait five seconds; it seems like an eternity, and most teachers are uncomfortable with a three to five-second silence. To be effective in asking questions you need to be willing to be uncomfortable and then to train yourself by counting off the seconds to yourself (paragraph quoted or paraphrased from Martin, 1980).

Call on Students Systematically

When you call on students, have a system. Over several class periods, make sure to call on everyone. Vary your system so that students don't anticipate when they'll be called. For example, don't always start at the back or front. Especially notice who you are not calling on.

Use Team Procedures

Use one or two minute team activities to involve students. All the team procedures discussed in Chapter 11—write-pair-share, think-pair-share, sentence completion, and round-robin—can be used to have students process material you've presented.

Have Students Make Concept Maps or Other Graphic Organizers

If students aren't getting the concepts and how they relate, consider having students make concept maps or other graphic organizers. Concept maps are especially good for summative activities, both to provide practice and to allow you to evaluate where students are understanding and where they are having problems. Other graphic organizers students can make include outlines, posters, word webs, flowcharts, and timelines. Any of these can be done individually or as a team of two or more.

Teach, Practice, and Monitor Note Taking

If you want students to take notes, teach effective note-taking procedures. Don't bother if you don't want to take the time to follow up on note taking, because the students who most need to learn and practice note taking won't do it. As the saying goes, it's not what you expect, it's what you inspect.

Someone once described college as a place where the notes of the professor pass to the notes of the students without passing through the mind of either. Note taking based on this model is a waste of time. If you want to use note taking, show students how to take notes, build note taking into the structure of the class, and provide accountability for note taking.

HAVE STUDENTS PUT NOTES IN THEIR OWN WORDS

While there may be exceptions, students benefit from putting what they understand into their own words. Merely copying what is on the board or writing down what the teacher says will not do much good. Note taking itself is an action schema that requires much practice. Also, as in learning almost every significant skill, learning conversations with peers and teachers can be helpful. Give student teams of two time to compare what they have put into their notes. Help students format their notes so that they can make sense of them when they go to use those notes days, weeks, or months later. You can find information on note taking online.

Reward Students Who Do a Good Job

Rewards are a way of creating accountability. Give a grade or extra credit for note taking to provide accountability and reward. Another way of motivating and rewarding students is to let them use their own written notes (and only their own written notes) on some quizzes and tests.

STAND-UP SKILLS: CONNECTING WITH STUDENTS

Stand-up skills help you connect with students. To the extent that you have already connected with students, you will find it easier to do behaviors in the sections below. Pick one behavior you want to work on. You will know what this behavior is because this is the behavior you feel uncomfortable reading about. That's how you know you need to work on it. Invite a colleague or videotape yourself to check your presentation skills. If you can get permission, also videotape student responses. Don't avoid doing it because it makes you uncomfortable.

To Increase Withitness, Be Overprepared

"Withitness" is having eyes in the back of your head—that is, being aware of what's going on in class (Kounin, 1970). You can develop it by being overprepared. The more prepared you are, the more you can focus on students. Your ability to monitor student response is the key that will make you effective in the long run. When you overprepare, you increase your presentation skills. Eventually, the skills you acquire become habitual. The better prepared you are, the more free and spontaneous you can be.

The age of the students, size of the room, room acoustics, culture of the group, and especially your delivery all go into the mix of what will hold your students' attention. When you pay attention to your listeners, you become aware of when you have them and when you're losing them.

Take Stage

When you speak to your group, "take stage" as a director would say to an actor who needs to be encouraged to be the center of attention for a moment. We can argue about whether teachers should be performers, but presenting is performing. Projecting enthusiasm to the back of a classroom, a gym, or a band room is different from speaking to a friend over coffee. Don't be afraid to be dramatic. Show enthusiasm. Ham it up. If you never feel silly in your stand-up teaching, you're not doing enough. We've all said, "I'm not here to be an entertainer!"—which is certainly true—but at the same time, presenting *is* performing. If you feel like you're doing too much, you're probably doing about the right amount.

Speak Loudly Enough to Be Easily Heard— or Students Will Tune Out

We speak the way we hear modeled, and what we hear modeled on TV and in movies is a conversational tone. Entertainers have something we don't have—microphones. Speaking loudly enough to be easily heard doesn't feel natural, but we need to do it anyway. Unless your class is very quiet or very small or the acoustics are very good, you need to speak more loudly than seems reasonable (unless you are a naturally loud talker). For a very quiet teacher, what seems like shouting may be just about right in a normal classroom.

If you don't think you're too loud, you're probably not loud enough. Listening to someone who talks very softly is an enormous effort, and even most adults will tune out after a short time. Young students will tune out almost immediately. On the other hand, a loud, pressuring voice is also difficult to listen to. Teachers who feel they are losing their students may speak very loudly as if to stun them into listening and behaving. Pay attention to the students: They will let you know by their nonverbal behavior if they are listening and paying attention. If they are not, do something different.

Move and Make Eye Contact

You don't need to be glued to one spot or even to the front of the room. Especially since you can't see what every student is doing from the front, move around the room. Eye contact allows you to connect and to see how the class is responding. Are they paying attention?

Breathe, Relax, Smile

Human beings learn more when they're attentive and relaxed; by being relaxed you encourage students to be more attentive and relaxed. You also need to be energized as well as relaxed. On the other hand, you don't need to tell jokes or be funny unless that is your style. It's enough to enjoy yourself and let the students know that you enjoy teaching them through your nonverbal behavior. You and they will be less defensive, more attentive, less likely to engage in power struggles, and better able to learn.

Be Positive, Be Encouraging

Be positive and encouraging even when you don't feel like it. As with all behavior, no matter how uncomfortable a behavior might feel, the more you do it, the more comfortable you become. Do what's effective even when you don't feel like it. Do it because you want to reach the students. There is nothing phony about being cheerful and enthusiastic when you don't feel like it; you are choosing to be cheerful for the sake of the students. And, as you act more cheerful and enthusiastic, you will feel more cheerful and enthusiastic.

FINAL THOUGHTS

Having made the case for connecting with students and involving them in learning, it's important to say that involving students in activities is not a magical technique that solves all problems. Using scoring guides, practice, team learning, conversation, and direct instruction needs to take place within the context of observing, reflecting, and making decisions about what's working and what isn't. No technique or learning method has ever been shown to be the final answer to having students learn and achieve at a high level. Techniques and methods always interact with the teachers using them and the students experiencing them.

Improving learning calls for a continual effort to be a detective, doing your best to observe and understand every possible detail of what you and your students are doing. Perhaps the word *observe* in the phrase "observe, reflect, decide" suggests a dispassionate and passive activity. A better phrase might be to "pay attention, reflect, decide." Paying attention to everything, reflecting on what we've observed, and then deciding what to do next is the road to learning to teach effectively. Pay attention and keep the ideas and practices in this book in the back of your mind. You'll learn everything you need to from paying attention. And then reflecting. And then deciding what to do next.

When I asked for advice on teaching from Herbert Brun, one of my teachers, he said: "Be hard on yourself, easy on the students." That has proven to be good advice. Being hard on myself has gotten better results than being hard on the students. I also remember that he was always willing to help students do better, and his standards were very, very high.

A SCRAP OF CONVERSATION

When I started presenting, I lectured to my shoes and I was resistant to the idea that teaching involves performing. This was not an effective attitude. I learned how to do the kind of direct instruction described in this chapter out of fear. I had the chance to do a one-day, all-day workshop on communication with a group of industry supervisors in southern Indiana for Purdue University. The director of adult education told me what to do: "Give them a burst of information for ten minutes, then have them do something."

I took his suggestions very seriously, since the evaluations I would receive would determine whether I would be rehired for this well-paying gig. I created more thorough lesson plans than I had ever done—with fully written-out procedures on 4 × 6 file cards that I put into a small ring binder. By going all-out on planning, I learned more than I ever thought possible about direct instruction and about being prepared. I alternated lecturing for about ten minutes and then involving these tough-minded first-line supervisors in an activity.

At the end of the day, they filled out the evaluations and rated the learning experience very highly. From this, I learned that activity-based learning works just as well with adults as it does with children. I learned that regardless of the age of your classes, if you want students to listen, involve them in your presentations. I used the little ring binder on many more occasions and still have it thirty-five years later.

CONCLUSION

Presenting is an opportunity to incorporate many different forms of involvement. If you monitor your students you will quickly learn how long you can talk before you start to lose them. Plan to involve them before you lose them.

In Chapter 1, we began with the theme of focusing on big ideas and key skills. Involving students more effectively always involves making choices about what to cut. There isn't time to present everything if students are going to learn the key skills and ideas in depth.

Previous chapters have discussed practice and revision in detail; the point to be made here is that modeling and practice of skills can and should be incorporated into presentations. It's too easy to assume that students can practice afterward or for homework, but the opportunity for students to make connections has already been lost.

The tension between choosing more presentation or more practice is part of the job. We won't ever get the mix perfect, but if our goal is to make sure students learn key skills and ideas, we will make our decisions with the goal of maximizing learning in mind. To be sure, involving students more actively may require you to cut back on the amount of information you present, but the more students process what you do present, the more they will learn.

Q & A

Q. *I tried a more active approach with my students. I don't have time to cover the material if I involve students more.*
A. Quite true. If you involve students in deep learning, you won't be able to cover as much material by presenting. But if motivation and learning increase, you may be able to cover the material in other ways.

Q. *Won't I lose control if I am relaxed?*
A. Teachers tend to lose control when they try too hard to be liked or when they try to be like their students. You're the adult; be relaxed and enjoy what you're doing as the adult in the room.

Q. *Isn't it better to avoid lecturing? I try never to lecture.*
A. There's always a mix between presenting and involving students. Even if you don't lecture, there are times when you need to orient students to what they're going to be doing—and they need to listen.

ADDITIONAL RESOURCES

Wiggins, G., & McTighe, J. (2005). *Understanding by design* (Expanded 2nd ed.). Upper Saddle River, NJ: Pearson/Merrill Prentice Hall.

If you want to go more deeply into the approach of designing backward from big ideas and skills, get this book. Wiggins and McTighe invented the understanding by design approach. This book is short (120 pages), but its templates and examples are very detailed and require deep thinking to apply to your lessons and units. An excellent guide to planning backward from what you want to achieve. Very clear and practical; Wiggins and McTighe have thought through every aspect of the ideas and practices they advocate.

Afterword

Our most productive times are often when we are having a conversation—especially when listening and observing. Listening and observing enables us to do the detective work that results in figuring out what others think, want, and need—and what we can do so that change occurs. I would have preferred to have had a conversation with you about your joys and concerns as a teacher, especially your immediate concerns with specific situations and specific students, parents, fellow teachers, or administrators.

One way to be more effective is to pay attention to procedures. Almost everything we do is a procedure—a set of behaviors we use over and over to deal with people and things—including the challenges of learning and deepening the key skills and big ideas each of us, teacher or student, needs to succeed. Teaching and learning are all about details, and the details of learning are embodied in the procedures we and our students use. Procedures free us to pay attention to what is around us, to think, to have conversations, to be creative. Once we become aware that we live in a sea of procedures and that those procedures can be designed and redesigned, we have a powerful way of using the fruit of observation and conversation.

Now that you are finished reading, consider rereading, maybe a paragraph at a time. Go a little deeper; reflect a little more on where you need to be more of a detective, where you need to pay attention, observe, and have conversations. Paying attention and having conversations are the two processes that can best help us develop our skills as teachers and as human beings.

References

Ainsworth, L. (2017, April 6). Priority standards: The power of focus. Website. https://www.larryainsworth.com/blog/priority-standards-the-power-of-focus/

Anderson, L. (2001). *A taxonomy for learning, teaching, and assessing: A revision of Bloom's taxonomy of educational objectives*. New York, NY: Longman.

Angelo, T. A., & Cross, K. P. (1993). *Classroom assessment techniques: A handbook for college teachers* (2nd ed.). San Francisco, CA: Jossey-Bass.

Au, K. H. (1998). Social constructivism and the school literacy learning of students of diverse backgrounds. *Journal of Literacy Research, 30*(2), 297–319.

Barkley, E. F., Cross, K. P., & Major, C. H. (2005). *Collaborative learning techniques: A handbook for college faculty*. San Francisco, CA: Jossey-Bass.

Baron P. (2018). Heterarchical reflexive conversational teaching and learning as a vehicle for ethical engineering curriculum design. *Constructivist Foundations 13*(3): 309–319. http://constructivist.info/13/3/309

Berger, R. (2003). *An ethic of excellence*. Portsmouth, NH: Heinemann.

Bloom, B. S. (1984). *Taxonomy of educational objectives. Book 1: Cognitive domain* (2nd ed.). Boston, MA: Addison Wesley.

Brookfield, S. D. (1991). *Developing critical thinkers*. San Francisco, CA: Jossey-Bass.

Brookfield, S. D. (1995). *Becoming a critically reflective teacher*. San Francisco, CA: Jossey-Bass.

Brookfield, S. D. (2006). *The skillful teacher: On technique, trust, and responsiveness in the classroom* (2nd ed.). San Francisco, CA: Jossey-Bass.

Browne, M. N, & Keeley, S. M. (2014). *Asking the right questions: A guide to critical thinking* (11th ed.). London, UK: Longman.

Bruner, J. S. (1960). *The process of education*. Cambridge, MA: Harvard University Press.

Bruner, J. S. (1961). The act of discovery. *Harvard Educational Review, 31*, 21–32.

Chavis, D. M., & Pretty, G. (1999). Sense of community: Advances in measurement and application. *Journal of Community Psychology, 27*(6), 635–642.

Cawelti, G. (Ed.). (2004). *Handbook of research on improving student achievement* (3rd ed.). Alexandria, VA: Educational Research Service.

Colvin, G. (2010). *Talent is overrated: What really separates world-class performers from everybody else.* New York, NY: Portfolio Trade.

Council of Chief State School Officers (2019). Common core state standards initiative. http://www.corestandards.org

Dewey, J. (2007). *Experience and education* (3rd ed.). New York, NY: Touchstone.

Dobson, K. S., & Dozois, D. J. (2019). *Handbook of cognitive-behavioral therapies* (4th ed.). New York, NY: Guilford Press.

Dreikurs, R. (1968). *Psychology in the classroom: A manual for teachers.* New York, NY: Harper & Row.

Dreikurs, R. (with Stolz, V.). (1991). *Children: The challenge* (reissued ed.). New York, NY: Plume.

Dreikurs, R. (2012). *Social equality: The challenge of today.* Chicago, IL: Adler School of Professional Psychology.

Dreikurs, R., Grunwald, B., & Pepper, F. (1998). *Maintaining sanity in the classroom* (2nd ed.). Philadelphia, PA: Taylor & Francis.

Duffy, T. M., & Cunningham, D. J. (1996). Constructivism: Implications for the design and delivery of instruction. In D. H. Jonassen (Ed.), *Handbook of research on educational communications and technology* (pp. 170–198). New York, NY: Scholastic.

Dweck, C. S. (2007). *Mindset: The new psychology of success—How we can learn to fulfill our potential.* New York, NY: Ballantine Books.

Ellis, A. (1975). *A new guide to rational living.* Englewood Cliffs, NJ: Prentice-Hall.

Ellis, A. (1977). *Reason and emotion in psychotherapy.* Secaucus, NJ: Citadel Press.

Ellis, A. (1978). *How to raise an emotionally healthy, happy child.* Hollywood, CA: Wilshire.

Ellis, A, & MacLaren, C. (2005). *Rational emotive behavior therapy: A therapist's guide.* Atascadaro, CA: Impact.

Esquith, R. (2007). *Teach like your hair's on fire: The methods and madness inside room 56.* New York, NY: Penguin Books.

Foerster, H. von. (2014). *The beginning of heaven and earth has no name: Seven days with second-order cybernetics* (A. Muller & K. H. Muller, Eds.; & E. Rooks & M. Kasenbacher, Trans.). New York, NY: Fordham University Press.

Foerster, H. von, & Poerksen, B. (2002). *Understanding systems: Conversations on epistemology and ethics* (K. Leube, Trans.). New York, NY: Kluwer Academic/Plenum.

Geert, D. T., & Volman, M. (2004). Critical thinking as a citizenship competence: Teaching strategies. *Learning and Instruction, 14*, 359–379.

Glasersfeld, E. von. (1995). *Radical constructivism: A way of knowing and learning.* London, UK: Falmer Press.

Glasser, W. (1969). *Schools without failure.* New York, NY: Harper & Row.

Glasser, W. (1975). *Reality therapy.* New York, NY: Harper Paperbacks.

Glasser, W. (1998a). *Choice theory in the classroom* (Rev. ed.). New York, NY: Harper Perennial.

Glasser, W. (1998b). *The quality school: Managing students without coercion* (3rd ed.). New York, NY: Harper Collins.

Glasser, W. (1999). *Choice theory: A new psychology of personal freedom.* New York, NY: Harper Perennial.

Glasser, W. (2001). *Counseling with choice theory: The new reality therapy.* New York, NY: Harper Paperbacks.

Glasser, W. (2006). *Every student can succeed.* Temecula, CA: Black Forest Press.

Gordon, T., & Birch, N. (2003). *T.E.T.: Teacher effectiveness training.* New York, NY: Three Rivers Press.

Greeley, K. (2001). *"Why fly that way?" Linking community and academic achievement.* New York, NY: Teachers College Press.

Gronlund, N. E., & Waugh, C. K. (2009). *Assessment of student achievement* (9th ed.). Upper Saddle River, NJ: Pearson.

Irby, B., Brown, G. H., LarAlecio, R., & Jackson, S. A. (Eds.). (2013). *Handbook of educational theories.* Charlotte, NC: Information Age Publishing.

Johnson, D. W., Johnson R. T., & Holubec, E. (1994). *The circles of learning.* Alexandria, VA: Association for Supervision & Curriculum Development.

Johnson, D. W., Johnson R. T., & Holubec, E. (2007). *The nuts and bolts of cooperative learning* (2nd ed.). Minneapolis, MN: Interaction Book Company.

Kagan, S., & Kagan, M. (2017). *Kagan cooperative learning.* San Clemente, CA: Kagan.

Kamii, C., & Ewing, J. K. (2012). Basing teaching on Piaget's constructivism. *Childhood Education, 72*(5), 260–264.

Kounin, J. S. (1970). *Discipline and group management in classrooms.* New York, NY: Holt, Rinehart & Winston.

Lyman, F. (1987). Think-pair-share. *MAA-CIE Cooperative News, 1*, 1–2.

McTighe, J., & Wiggins, G. (2012). *Understanding by design framework.* Alexandria, VA: ASCD. https://www.ascd.org/ASCD/pdf/siteASCD/publications/UbD_WhitePaper0312.pdf

Martin, R. J. (1980). *Teaching through encouragement.* Englewood Cliffs, NJ: Prentice-Hall.

Martin, R. J. (1983). *A skills and strategies handbook for dealing with people.* Englewood Cliffs, NJ: Prentice-Hall.

Martin R. J. (2018). Are we professors if no one is learning? Changing university education. *Constructivist Foundations, 13*(3): 329–330. http://constructivist.info/13/3/329

Maturana, H. R., & Varela, F. J. (1992). *The tree of knowledge: The biological roots of human understanding* (Rev. ed.). Boston, MA: Shambhala.

McMillan, D. W., & Chavis, D. M. (1986). Sense of community: A definition and theory. *Journal of Community Psychology, 14*(1), 6–23.

McMullin, R. E. (1999). *Cognitive therapy techniques* (2nd ed.). New York, NY: W. W. Norton.

McTighe, J. & Wiggins, G. (2012). *Understanding by design framework.* Alexandria, VA: ASCD. https://www.ascd.org/ASCD/pdf/siteASCD/publications/UbD_WhitePaper0312.pdf

Missouri State Department of Elementary & Secondary Education. (2012). *Missouri Professional Learning Communities Project*. Jefferson City, MO: Missouri Department of Elementary & Secondary Education. https://dese.mo.gov/quality-schools/school-improvement-initiatives/professional-learning-communities

Mooney, C. G. (2013). *Theories of childhood: An introduction to Dewey, Montessori, Erikson, Piaget & Vygotsky* (2nd ed.). St. Paul, MN: Redleaf Press.

Newmann, F., & Wehlage, G. (1993). Five standards of authentic instruction. *Educational Leadership, 50*, 8-12. http://www.learner.org/workshops/socialstudies/pdf/session6/6.AuthenticInstruction.pdf

Nosich, G. M. (2011). *Learning to think things through: A guide to critical thinking across the curriculum* (4th ed.). Upper Saddle River, NJ: Prentice-Hall.

Payne, R. (2005). *A framework for understanding poverty* (4th rev. ed.). Highlands, TX: Aha! Press.

Piaget, J. (1973). *To understand is to invent: The future of education*. New York, NY: Viking Press.

Piaget, J. (1975). *The child's conception of the world*. Totowa, NJ: Littlefield, Adams.

Pike, R. W. (2003). *Creative training techniques handbook: Tips, tactics, and how-to's for delivering effective training* (3rd ed.). Amherst, MA: Human Resource Development Press.

Rowe, M. B. (1974). Wait-time and rewards as instructional variables, their influence on language, logic, and fate control: Part 1. Fate control. *Journal of Research in Science Teaching, 11*, 81–94.

Schoen, D. A. (1984). *The reflective practitioner: How professionals think in action*. New York, NY: Basic Books.

Schwandt, T. A. (1994). Constructivist, interpretivist approaches to human inquiry. In N. K. Denzin & Y. S. Lincoln (Eds.), *Handbook of qualitative research* (pp. 118–137). Thousand Oaks, CA: Sage.

Simon, S., Howe, L., & Kirschenbaum, H. (1995). *Values clarification* (Rev. ed.). New York, NY: Grand Central Books.

Solomon, J. (2000). The changing perspective of constructivism: Science wars and children's creativity. In D. C. Phillips (Ed.), *Constructivism in education: Opinions and second opinions on controversial issues* (pp. 283–307). Chicago, IL: University of Chicago Press.

Spivey, N. N. (1997). *The constructivist metaphor: Reading, writing, and the making of meaning*. San Diego, CA: Academic Press.

Tishman, S., Perkins, D. N., & Jay, E. (1994). *The thinking classroom: Learning and teaching in a culture of thinking*. Upper Saddle River, NJ: Pearson.

Vygotsky, L. S. (1978). *Mind in society: The development of higher psychological processes*. Cambridge, MA: Harvard University Press.

Vygotsky, L. (1986). *Thought and language*. Cambridge, MA: MIT Press.

Wexler, N. (2019). *The knowledge gap: The hidden cause of America's broken educational system—and how to fix it*. New York, NY: Avery.

Wigginton, E. (1972). *The foxfire book*. Garden City, NY: Anchor Books.

Wigginton, E. (1973). *Foxfire 2*. Garden City, NY: Anchor Books.

Wiggington, E. (1974). *Foxfire 3*. Garden City, NY: Anchor Books.
Wiggins, G. (1991). Standards, not standardization: Evoking quality student work. *Educational Leadership*, *48*(5), 18–25.
Wiggins, G. (1993). *Assessing student performance: Exploring the purpose and limits of testing.* San Francisco, CA: Jossey-Bass.
Wiggins, G. (1994). Toward better report cards. *Educational Leadership, 52*(2), 28–37.
Wiggins, G. (1995). Designing performance assessment tasks. *Education Update*, *37*(6), 1–8.
Wiggins, G. (1996). Honesty and fairness: Toward better grading and reporting. In T. Guskey (Ed.), *Communicating Student Learning* (pp. 141–177). Alexandria, VA: Association for Supervision & Curriculum.
Wiggins, G. (1997, December/January). Practicing what we preach in designing authentic assessments. *Educational Leadership*, *54*(4), 18–25.
Wiggins, G. (2012). *What is understanding by design?* [Video]. YouTube. https://www.youtube.com/watch?v=WsDgfC3SjhM
Wiggins, G. (2013a). *Understanding by design (1 of 2)* [Video]. YouTube. https://www.youtube.com/watch?v=4isSHf3SBuQ
Wiggins, G. (2013b). *Understanding by design (2 of 2)* [Video]. YouTube. https://www.youtube.com/watch?v=vgNODvvsgxM
Wiggins, G., & McTighe, J. (2005). *Understanding by design* (Expanded 2nd ed.). Upper Saddle River, NJ: Pearson/Merrill Prentice Hall.
Wong, H. K., & Wong, R. (2018). *The first days of school: How to be an effective teacher* (5th ed.). Mountain View, CA: Harry K. Wong.

Index

accountability:
   and directions, 85; in notetaking, 140; in team learning, 101-102, 106–107, 114, 123
achievement, 6, 17, 22, 29, 46, 58, 92, 103, 105, 127.
   See also Handbook of Research on Improving Student Achievement
   See also high stakes testing
activities, summative, 61, 128, 131, 140.
   See also projects
advance organizers, 137
agency, 29, 31–32, 92, 120
anxiety, 19–20, 58, 86

basic needs, 26–31, 36
belonging as a basic need, 17–18, 23, 26, 28-30, 36, 103, 131
best practice, xiv–xv, 56
big ideas and key skills:
   conversation in learning, 125–126, 129–130, 133; designing learning for, 5, 37–46, 49-56, 81; identifying, 41–42; practicing, 6–7, 21, 39, 44, 50, 91, 101–102, 105–106, 110; projects for learning, 94, 99; scoring guides for learning, 57, 59–65; using presentation to teach, 137–138, 144–145, 147; using teams in learning, 102, 113–115, 118–119, 123.
   See also lesson and unit plans
   See also planning

calling on students, 102, 133, 139.
   See also conversation
changes, small. *See* small changes
checklists:
   getting to know students, 16; scoring guides, 60; warmups, 68, 69
choices:
   designing, 70, 73, 103, 120–121; helping students make, 21, 25–36, 125; teacher, 9, 43, 49, 144
closure activities, 109, 117, 132, 138–139
cognitive behavioral model, 2, 3
comfort zone, 13, 35, 52, 76, 81, 139, 141, 143
community:
   and academic achievement, 56; and belonging, 17–18; and learning, 17; and quality time, 18; build/develop, 16-18, 22, 105-106, 125–133.
   See also learning communities
   See also student neighborhoods and communities
concept mapping, 94, 97–98, 138, 140;

project plans for, 115-117
conflict, 17, 106, 123
connecting, 1–4, 7–9; as a door to change, 21; rationale for, 11; through getting to know students, 11–23; through helping students make choices, 25–36
content ideas and skills. *See* big ideas and key skills
conversation:
    about basic needs, 30–31; about quality work, 61–62; as quality time, 18; circles, 129–130; diagnosing learning problems, 90; guidelines/procedures for, 128–131; monopolizing, 130–131; rationale for, 125–128; time for, 22; to augment direct instruction, 131–132; to increase learning and build community, 125–133; with class, 15, 132; with individual students, 13, 14.
    See also big ideas and key skills, using conversation in learning
    See also right to pass
cooperative learning. *See* teams
core standards. *See* state standards
covering material, 9, 39, 42, 46, 55, 122, 145
crisis situations, 19
curriculum, 4, 30, 37, 41–43, 45, 55, 113.
    See also big ideas and key skills, identifying
    See also covering material
    See also high-stakes testing
    See also state standards

design of learning, 37–47.
    See also big ideas and key skills, designing for
detective, become a, 2, 41, 90, 143, 147
differentiation, 92, 106
difficult situations. See strategy, for difficult situations

direct instruction, 7, 135–136, 143–144; using conversation to augment, 131–133
directions, 81, 84–85.
    See also instructions
discipline, 32, 36, 85, 88.
    See also power struggles
discussion. *See* conversation

empathy, 11, 19, 35
encourage self, 7-8,
encouragement, 4, 7–8, 17–19, 21–22, 31, 72, 75, 77, 103, 106, 118, 142–143.
    See also praise
    See also rewards
evaluation:
    one-minute, 19–20; praise as, 69.
    See also scoring guides
    See also self-evaluation
    See also student products and performances
expectations, 8, 17, 35, 57, 72

fear. *See* motivation
freedom as a basic need, 26–30, 36, 103
fun as a basic need, 14, 20, 26–31, 36, 44, 69, 72
funds of knowledge, 41, 90–92, 118–119, 125–127, 133; new experiences, 31–32
groups, *See* teams
group discussion. *See* conversation

Glasser, William, 57, 123, 127, 129, 133; basic concepts, xiii–xiv; choice theory, 25–36; problem solving strategy, 32–34; resources, 36, 77, 123; responsibility and love, 18; quotations, 1, 37, 82, 101, 113, 125.
    See also basic needs
graphic organizers, 138, 140
guided instruction. *See* direct instruction

Handbook of Research on Improving Student Achievement, 56
high-stakes testing, 5, 37, 40–41, 45, 57, 110, 123

instruction:
  authentic, 65.
  See also direct instruction
instructions, 22, 51, 53–54, 57, 80–81, 84–85, 87, 111.
  See also directions
  See also procedures
involving, 1–9.
  See also presentation, involving students
  See also procedures
  See also strategies, for involving students
  See also teams

Kagan and Kagan, 85, 103, 111, 121, 123
key skills. *See* big ideas and key skills

learning:
  and culture, 6, 12, 21, 23, 91, 101, 103, 138, 141; and poverty, 6, 23
lecture. *See* presentation
lesson and unit plans, 49–56;
  as designs for learning, 49–50; for teaching big ideas and key skills, 50–52; lesson templates, 52–53; revising, lessons 54; week by week overview, 42–44.
  See also instructions
  See also planning
learning communities, 23, 103, 133

mastery approach, 91–93, 119
mental pictures, 26, 30–31, 70; and new experiences, 31–32
motivation, 9, 17, 93–94, 123, 133, 145;

acting despite feelings, 74–75; fear, 4, 20, 70, 75–76, 82; follows action, 67–77; strategies, 71–74
needs, basic. *See* basic needs
note taking, 140–141

objectives, 40, 43, 45, 137; higher-order, 64
outlines, 69, 94, 97, 137, 140
overprepare, 18, 141

plan B, 54
planning:
  plan backward, 37, 41; steps for teaching big ideas and key skills, 40–45; time blocks, 53–54, 115, 130.
  See also lesson and unit plans
power as a basic need, 26–30, 32–33, 36, 103
power struggles, 13, 34–35, 77, 142
practice, student. *See* student practice
praise, 14, 69
practice, 38–40, 46, 50–52, 70, 76; as an approach, 99; distributed, 93; learning through 89–100; tips for, 93; using teams for, 101–111.
  See also big ideas and key skills, practicing
  See also big ideas and key skills, score guides for learning
  See also procedures
practice tests, 116
Premacking, 72–73, 76, 93
preparation:
  student, 128, 131–132;
  teacher, 8, 19, 49, 82, 84–85, 101, 144.
  See also overprepare
presentation:
  eye contact, 142; involving students in, 135–145; organizing material,

136–137; speaking voice, 142; teacher skills, 141–143; ways to encourage attention, 137–138.
See also big ideas and key skills, using presentation to teach
See also overprepare
pressure, 20, 22, 28, 39, 76, 119
prior knowledge, 5, 38–39, 51, 90, 126
prior learning, 21, 137
problem solving, 32.
See also, strategy, problem solving
procedures 3, 51, 89, 96–98; teaching, 5–6, 79–88; rationale for, 80–81; round robin, 108–109; secrets for using, 81–82; sentence completion, 108; that help students organize, 86–87; think-pair-share, 108; write-pair-share, 107
projects:
dream, 45, 118–119; examples, 115–117; large, 118–122; planning, 113–122; summative, 94.
See also revising
prompts, 15, 20, 97

quality work, 1, 6, 32, 36, 57–59, 61–65, 98–99, 121, 125, 130
questions:
and wait time, 139; ask rather than tell 138; for evaluating, 19-20, 59, 89, 91, 139; for getting to know students, 15, 30; for review, 109, 117; for student problem choices, 33–34; on high-stakes testing, 41; structuring choices, 70, 97; student questions and answers, 50, 102, 122; to avoid, 13–14, 22
See also calling on students

reading, 40, 46, 50–51, 96, 99–100, 125–126, 128
reflective practitioner, xi, 2
reframing, 3, 17, 83, 119
revising:

assignments, 63; by students, 21, 62–63, 68, 94–97, 99–100, 125, 144; lessons 43–44, 53–54, 57–58, 119, 121; project plans, 121; students working in passes, 96–98
rewards, 14, 69, 141
right to pass, 130

scope and sequence, 45, 55
scoring guides:
examples of excellence, 61; guidelines, 60–61; having students use, 61–63; rationale, 57–58; steps for creating, 58–63
seating arrangements, 110
self-evaluation, 31, 36
self-regulation, 25, 29–32, 36, 51
semantic memory, 136
semantic organizers, 136
skills. See big ideas and key skills
slippage, 43
small changes, xiii–xv, 1–8, 21, 45, 75, 82
standards, state, See state standards
story form, using, 115, 138
state standards, 5, 37, 39–41, 45
strategies, 3; act, observe, reflect, choose, 2; as direction, 3; connecting with students, 12–22; first things first, 4; for conversation, 128–131; for designing lessons, 51–52; for difficult situations, 29, 34–35; for involving students, 21; going beyond present skills, 7; one new practice at a time, 9; reasonable expectations, 8.
See also motivation, strategies
student neighborhoods and communities, 15–16
student peer review, 62, 117
student products and performances, 58, 61, 64, 113–114, 118
student work, using examples of, 61–62, 64–65
student strengths, 11, 14, 71

student writing:
  editing and proofreading, 95–96;
  guidelines, 94–96.
  See also revising
  See also outlines
summative activities, 128, 131, 140.
  See also summative projects
summative projects, 61, 94
survival as a basic need, 26

teacher expertise, 2, 55, 109, 121
teacher intentions, 12–13, 17
teacher vision, 44–45
teaching to increase understanding. *See* big ideas and key skills
teams, 101–111, 113–123.
  and conversation, 102; as learning communities, 103; assessing activity risk, 106; benefits of, 102–103; building expertise, through practice, 109; guidelines for, 104–106; setting up, 105; structuring, 106.
  See also accountability
  See also big ideas and key skills, using teams in learning
  See also procedures
techniques. *See* strategies
  See also procedures
ten-minute commitments, 71–72
templates:
  basic needs, 30; lesson plan, 52–53; scoring guide, 59, 60; team project plan, 114; using for writing, 95.
  See also practice, using teams
themes, of the book, 3–8

wait time, 139
warm-up activities, 68–69
withitness, 141
writing. *See* student writing

About the Author

As a licensed psychologist, **Robert J. Martin** has worked in public schools with K–12 teachers and students, and in private practice with children, adolescents, families, as well as adults of all ages. He has taught classes and workshops for in-service teachers and for graduate and undergraduate students in educational psychology and counselor education for over four decades. He is Professor Emeritus of Education at Truman State University, Missouri.

www.ingramcontent.com/pod-product-compliance
Lightning Source LLC
Chambersburg PA
CBHW021843220426
43663CB00005B/386